Kingdoms at War

T.J. Dillingham

Publisher: Ralph Roberts
Editor: Pat Roberts
Cover Design: Ralph Roberts
Cover Art: Teddy Lynn Ledford

10 9 8 7 6 5 4 3 2 1

ISBN 1-57090-155-4

Mountain Church—a division of Creativity, Inc.—is a full–service publisher located at 65 Macedonia Road, Alexander NC 28701. Phone (828) 252–9515, Fax (828) 255–8719. For orders only: 1-800-472-0438. Visa and MasterCard accepted.

Mountain Church is distributed to the trade by **Midpoint Trade Books**, Inc., 27 West 20th Street, New York NY 10011, (212) 727-0190, (212) 727-0195 fax.

This book is also available on the Internet at **abooks.com.** Set your browser to **http://abooks.com** and enjoy the many fine values available there.

Contents

DEDICATIONS

To my Lord and Savior, my beloved Jesus Christ,
without whom I am nothing.

To the best gift, friend, and helpmate ever granted a
wandering soul, my wife Renée!
Her unwavering motivation and encouragement has
propelled me to the completion of this task.

To my three sons: Kyle, Jared, and Eric.

PREFACE

thought

It is with much trepidation, and vigilant prayer that I undertake the responsibility of writing this book. If I had my rathers, when it comes to writing, I would rather not. Upon reading my writing some would rather I hadn't! All kidding aside, I had always though there were more gifted writers than I who would be better suited for presenting this material. However through my eighteen years of study and research of the subject at hand, I found no one whom completely explained spiritual warfare or fully exposed Satan's kingdom.

As I have researched and studied over these years, I have learned that any time you expose Satan's kingdom there will be war. I have smelled the stench of spiritual death as I lay in the trenches of war. I have felt the fiery darts of hell, as I have struggled to pull down the strongholds of the soul. At times I have even faltered in holding the shield of faith while grappling with guilt and shame. My fingernails hold the stains of clinging to desolation; due to my apparent lack of knowledge of the King, and I have discovered the biggest obstacle the graces of God must overcome is the biblical illiteracy of the ones who claim to love Him most. As we shall learn God's people perish daily for a lack of knowledge.

My procrastination is not a retreating from duty, or the charge set before me. My hesitation comes not of fear of mine enemies for they have been vanquished at the foot of the cross of Jesus Christ! However, completely exposing the strategies of Satan's kingdom, and explaining spiritual warfare on a practical plain is a daunting task. Herein lies my hesitation. I desired this book to be more than theory. I prayed daily for it to be a practical soldier's handbook for combating the enemy. This took much prayer, vast warfare, and the expense of much time. To think God almighty, creator of heaven and earth would commission such an unworthy vessel as I to expose Satan's kingdom is a humbling thought indeed.

This book is basically written towards the saved in Christ, for only they will understand its material and find it most useful. As I sit down to undertake the task of writing, I come cognitively aware of the different faith levels that will grace the pages of this book. It is my desire and intent to meet the need of all those in the body of Christ. Some will close their mind to these words, yet others may read to find fault. I can testify that this book came through much warfare and great trials and tribulation. God knows the heart from whence these words are written. Read them prayerfully and carefully. Test them to see if the fruit it bears is good. If you indeed find them to be good, then praise God for He is worthy. For without Christ no fruit is possible. All good that may come of this book is of Christ and Christ alone.

1

The Need

CHURCH BOMBING–20 KILLED

The First Baptist Church on Main Street exploded Sunday morning during the eleven o'clock worship service. By early afternoon, twenty people were reported dead at the St. Jude Hospital and hundreds more were wounded. Some received just minor scrapes and bruises, others required stitches. Local authorities have said that an anti-Christ terrorist group has claimed responsibility. The group vowed that the bombings will continue until the Christian voice is stamped out and any individual or organization that proclaims the name of Jesus Christ will be targeted.

Can you imagine waking up Monday morning to this headline in your local paper? What thoughts would run through your mind upon reading such an article? Would it be one of disbelief, or perhaps shock? Would you be gripped with fear, for the realization that it could have been your church? Maybe you would be rocked with anger at the thought that someone would do such a thing to the house of God. Regardless of the thoughts running through your mind, I'm confident that the

Christian community would start asking some serious questions. They're most likely to ask, what kind of weapons are
this terrorist group using? They might ask, how well trained
are they, and how well organized? You might be thinking they
would ask how could we protect our families, our churches,
and ourselves? All of these are good questions that would need
to be asked and addressed under such circumstances.

Well, I have some good news and some bad news! You're
right, let's go with the good news first. Well as you can guess, the
bombing in this bogus article didn't really happen. It was written
to bring home a point. Which brings us to the bad news. There is
a terrorist army out there that has targeted your churches, communities, families, and yes that's right, your very souls. What
makes this bad news is nobody is asking the questions. You know
the ones, what kind of weapons are they using? How well trained
are they? How well organized is their army? More importantly
how can we protect our families, churches, and ourselves?

That army belongs to none other than the kingdom of Satan!
Despite what you might think, Satan isn't omnipresent or om-
nipotent! Satan is not everywhere all the time. However one third
of a numberless amount of angels fell with Satan! That's a lot of
angels, but don't panic just yet! That leaves two-thirds of a numberless amount assigned to the Kingdom of God. Amen! Satan,
just like every other created thing in God's universe, is subject to
the principles and laws that govern that universe. Satan is limited
in authority and power by God as can clearly be seen in Scripture. Satan, however, will still utilize those fallen angels under his
control to come against the Kingdom of Heaven.

Even though Colossians 2:15 tells us that Jesus has already
won the victory, we still see so many Bible believing Christians
living defeated and deflated lives? We find so many Christian have
become the sour pickle on God's banquet table of life. All one has
to do is look around as the death toll rises from the hate and violence growing in our children and see something is dreadfully
wrong with this picture. The world is asking where is God if not
outright seeking a God in some form or fashion. Whether it is
through tarot cards, astrology, humanism, cults and the occult, or
whatever. God's answer is, "I am in the church." You see God

hasn't gone way from the church; the church has fallen away from God. The church has failed to show the wisdom of God as commanded in Ephesians 3:10 which states "To the intent that now unto the principalities and powers in heavenly places might be known by the church the manifold wisdom of God."

You know it is hard to show wisdom from the bottom of destruction. Hosea 4:6 tells us that God's people are destroyed for a lack of knowledge. That can better be expressed by saying, a lack of understanding the truth. How did the people in Hosea's day come to that position? Was the knowledge or truth not available? We find the answer in the rest of that scripture, "because they rejected the knowledge." The church finds itself in the same condition today. We have gotten so grounded in the politics and traditions of men that we have left God out of the equation. We have rejected truth and replaced it with traditions of men. A wise old pastor told me one time, "that the most difficult thing for the truth of the word of God to overcome is traditions of men." It seems we are more satisfied with the regurgitated food from the pulpit than feasting on the living word of truth.

It appears the church is more concerned about the number of people saved than the number of discipled, trained soldiers capable of fighting the good fight. This is like the Army being more concerned with the number of recruits than the number of trained soldiers ready to fight. An army like that doesn't survive long. It's no wonder we find the church trying to hold back the gates of hell, instead of the other way around. "And I say also unto thee, that thou art Peter, and upon this rock I will build my church; and the gates of hell shall not prevail against it" (Matt. 16:18).

The biggest problem the church faces today is biblical illiteracy. Christians just don't know the Bible! We know about its stories but not the principles we are to live by and use to defeat the powers of darkness. Matthew Henry in his commentary states it so beautifully for us: "Ignorance is so far from being the mother of devotion that it is the mother of destruction." We cannot be spiritually raised on Cliff Notes and sound bytes. We must expand our knowledge of the word of God.

No longer can the regurgitated bread from the pulpits of America sustain our spiritual walk. The next time you go to church ask someone to name one of the six foundation principles of Christ. In case you don't know them yourself, they are listed in Hebrews 6:1-2. If you didn't know them don't feel bad, most Christians don't. In fact I went to a pastors' conference and asked one hundred pastors to name the six principles. Only one of those hundred could do that. It's really not their fault, because they are not taught in seminary. Seminaries are so busy teaching church growth principles, they sometimes fail to teach God's principles. It should then be no surprise to find Christians who do not understand the concept of dying to yourself daily. We don't know why we should die, how do we die, and who benefits from that death. When a problem arises we are told to have faith. But no one tells us how to have faith, a real life changing practical faith that can be applied to our daily lives. They just say you've got to have faith. I could go on for pages with these examples.

We can agree that we must, as commanded by scripture, study to show ourselves approved. Brothers and sisters in Christ; this book is no different. You cannot take the words that are before you as ultimate truth. You must study the material for yourself. See if it lines up with the truth of God's word. Try it and see if the fruit it bears in your life is good. So the first need is to seek knowledge from the word of God. Reject not its truths! As you proceed through these pages my prayer for you is that you will grow in grace and knowledge of the truth of Jesus Christ.

We find the second need in Ephesians 6:11. Here God's word is telling us to "stand against the wiles of the Devil." The word wiles is a Greek word *methodeias*, meaning plans or schemes, which he uses to entrap us. Moses was told to "vex the Midianites, and smite them" (Num. 25:17). The word vex comes from the word *tsarar* which means to bind, to tie up, and to shut up; to show hostility toward, or to treat with enmity. Why did God use such a harsh word? Verse 18 gives us the answer. "For they vex you with there wiles, wherewith they have beguiled you in the matter of Peor, and in the matter of Cozbi, the daughter of a Prince of Midian, their sister, which was slain in the day of the plague for Peor's sake." It seems that the Midianites through their plans and schemes were destroying God's people. They were trying to shut God's people up. They were trying to get God's people to accept the way of Peor and Cozbi, which God knew would bring plagues upon his people. Satan through his plans and schemes is trying to accomplish the same task today in God's people. Just like Moses, we should vex the kingdom of Satan in our lives and our families. We should leave nothing of the kingdom of Satan standing.

The problem today as already stated is that Christians haven't been taught the Bible. So we don't know the devil's plans and schemes. In fact we know very little about our greatest enemy. A great strategist once said, "The greatest way to defeat your enemy is to know everything about them." We should know the kingdom of Satan's strengths in order to avoid them. You should know their weaknesses, and take advantage of those weaknesses. The majority of Christians don't even know their own strengths and weaknesses let alone those of Satan's kingdom. We will not only expose Satan's kingdom in this book, but also go a long way in exposing his army's tactics and strategies. Upon completion you will be able to predict that army's movements against you, your families, and your churches.

The majority of people who are introduced to the saving grace of Jesus Christ are not informed that he is not only a savior but also a king. These young Christians are not told that they have enlisted in a kingdom that is in the middle of a war. They are not trained or properly equipped for warfare. So the majority find no lasting success in the Christian way of life. Christians should be trained in conduct and duty. We should teach them to be loyal and trustworthy. We should instruct them in the laws and principles that govern God's kingdom. We should share with them the rewards and punishments. When they know and understand well enough to follow along, then teach them how to operate in the kingdom of Jesus Christ (Exod. 18:20).

Let me give you an example of what happens in churches today. (Note: there are exceptions to every rule.) An individual comes forward wanting salvation, the pastor asks a few questions, and the church accepts this new Christian. Hopefully he goes on to baptism. That is often where the church involvement ends. Yes, we encourage them to go to church and to come to our programs. However what happens when the individual has a problem? What happens when a walk becomes a crawl? Does the church run to him, offering restoration and healing to this new Christian? Most honest churchgoers would have to say no. Typically what most Christians do is sit back in their pew watching and waiting for the new Christian to make a mistake then the gossiping and criticizing starts. In a nutshell they execute the new Christian. We are the only army in the world that executes its wounded. This scenario would be likened to a man enlisting in the army this morning, given a gun this afternoon, and put on the battlefield the next day. How long do you think that soldier would survive in that war? Not long! What's going to happen when word gets back to the civilian population as to the fate of this soldier? Do you think they're going to rush out and enlist in that army? Not likely!

A soldier without training cannot stand up against one opponent, yet most Christians are going against a hundred opponents. To send these foundling Christians out to war without teaching them is called abandoning them. This is for the most part what we have done to young Christians. Yes, we have wonderful programs and church attendance is at an all-time high. Yet we still find Christians who are biblically illiterate, with no real understanding of how to operate in the kingdom of God. Most Christians have no real understanding of their base of operation. No real comprehension of what the armor looks like let alone how to wear it and function in it. Hosea doesn't say that God's people are being destroyed for a lack of programs. It doesn't even say they are being destroyed for a lack of emotion. We are not dying from either of these for we have plenty of both of those to go around. No, we are dying from lack of knowledge based on the truth of God's word.

We must gain knowledge of how the kingdom of Heaven functions and operates. If the Spirit of God bids us to come unto the Father through Christ then we can surely know that He bids us to come into a successful place in that kingdom. Amen! Success starts as we walk through the door of knowledge, the word of God. Once within the room we obtain application. Application brings wisdom. A simple formula to remember to gain wisdom from God is:

Knowledge + Application = Wisdom

If we put application to our worldly knowledge it brings a worldly wisdom that leads to death. On the other hand if we have biblical knowledge sprinkled with application it brings godly wisdom that leads to life.

In these pages we will not only expose the enemy, but also open the doors to the kingdom of Heaven. We will look at the Holy Spirit's base of operation, and how we function in that base. We will examine the weapons of our warfare.

The last area of need that we will discuss is the collective body of believers called the church. The house of God is very divided today, and a house divided cannot stand. We must understand the true purpose of the church and function within that purpose. We will delve deeply into that purpose. We will discuss how to avoid what I call non-winnable wars. We will look at the art of strategically thinking. We will draw upon the principle of unity through the bond of peace. We will even look upon the hedge of protection through spiritual gifts.

Now find you a quiet place with plenty of room for pen and paper. Maybe some reference books, and come march with us on the War Between the Kingdoms.

2

The Enemy Exposed

For we wrestle not against flesh and blood, but against principalities, against powers, against the rulers of the darkness of this world, against spiritual wickedness in high places. Eph 6:12 KJV

Most people do not believe in a real Satan or that hell is a literal place! In fact only thirty-four percent of Americans believe in Satan and Hell. Most people believe that Satan is just a name we put on evil. They think, that if you believe in Satan and hell you are taking this God stuff too seriously. In fact we don't find the statistics much better in the church world. There was a survey done in which they found that only forty-five percent of church going Christians believed in a real Satan. That's less than half that believe in a real Satan and of that half their understanding of Satan is sketchy at best. We are told to "stand against the wiles of the devil" (Eph 6:11 KJV). How can we do this when half of us Christians don't believe in Satan and the other half really don't know Satan let alone the wiles of Satan? Think about this for a moment, if the enemy can convince us that he doesn't exist, then he has won half the battle.

You cannot believe in God, Jesus or the work of the Holy Spirit and not also believe in a real person called Satan. If Satan is not real and we cannot believe in a real Spirit person called Satan; then our Lord Jesus Christ would have had been a flake. You see Jesus spoke to him directly by name. Now if anyone speaks directly to a force and calls that force by name, they would have to be considered a flake. I know, as well as you should that Jesus was no flake! Jesus Christ knew full well whom He was addressing, and that being the archenemy of our souls. In pursuing an understanding the enemy let's start with what Satan is not.

We know that Satan is not all-powerful. He can't leap a tall building in a single bound, or go faster than a speeding bullet. He can't stop a freight train. That's right Satan isn't some super spirit that can destroy you at will. Satan is not the lone wolf looking for someone to eat. If you remember, Satan has one third of the angels under his authority. I wish I had space to share how Satan got his start and how he convinced those angels to rebel. As my father likes to say "there is a time and place for everything." Maybe in the next book we can go there. We should know this, when the Bible talks about Satan it is referring not only to the personage of Satan himself but the fallen angels with him that make up the kingdom of Satan. When we talk about Satan, we are really talking about his kingdom and/or his army.

Knowing that Satan has an army, we must understand the battle we are engaged in. Jesus does not want us defeated through ignorance of the fact that Satan has an army with devices (2 Cor. 2:11). When you came to the saving grace of Jesus Christ you by default became an enemy of the army of Satan. When you said I accept the blood of Jesus Christ, you in essence were raising your right hand and swearing into the Army of the Kingdom of Heaven. In fact you must be made aware of the reality that you came into a kingdom at war. The minute you took on the new birth through the power of the Holy Spirit you became a target of the enemy.

I know of no war that is pretty and this war we are engaged in is no exception. This battle is for keeps. The stakes are high indeed. The Greek word used in Ephesians 6:12 that is translated wrestle is *pale*, which means hand to hand combat. It means an enemy that will go to the uttermost in combat to achieve victory even if it means death. Make no mistake my friends the battle you are engaged in is not pretty. The enemy is not trying to just hinder you here or there. No! The enemy is trying to destroy you, and or subdue you to surrender your will to him. According to 1 Peter 5:8, we have been placed in a battle: "be sober, be vigilant, [be alert]; because your adversary the devil, is a roaring lion, walketh about, seeking whom he may devour" or totally consume. Satan does not just want to pick a fight with you. The kingdom of Satan wants to totally eliminate you. Satan wants to eliminate your testimony. He wants to eliminate your marriage, and your relationships. Make no mistake he wants to destroy every part of your life in Christ.

My father was in the Vietnam conflict, and he told me that the hardest part of that war was not knowing who your enemy was. He said you just didn't know if that little boy coming up to you for candy really wanted candy or if he had grenades strapped under his shirt to kill you. It is hard to defeat an enemy you don't know. I sometimes think this is where most Christians find themselves. They really don't know the enemy so we end up fighting among ourselves more often than not. Our fight is not with each other! No, it's not with the next-door neighbor you're mad at. It is not your wife, husband, children, or any other fleshly person. It plainly states here in Ephesians that we do not fight against flesh and blood. With all of that said let us expose this enemy kingdom in the light of the word of God that we may not be found ignorant of its devices.

We know from scripture that Satan is a counterfeiter. Satan's kingdom is trying to counterfeit the kingdom of Heaven. We also know that God is a God of order, and His kingdom has a structure and authority. Likewise Satan's kingdom also has structure and a sense of authority. Satan's kingdom operates like a large army. It has all the elements and structure of an army. Let's take a close look at Satan's army.

Let's go straight to the source for our information and look in Ephesians 6:12. "For we wrestle not against flesh and blood, but against (1) **principalities**, against (2) **powers**, against the (3) **rulers of the darkness of this world**, against (4) **spiritual wickedness in high places**" (KJV).

What I find so amazing about this passage it the fact that our arch enemy is displayed in full battle gear marching against us. Notice Paul doesn't present the kingdom of Satan in a feeble or weak way. We see here Paul presenting the Christian with the worst of it. Giving us the plain and simple truth. Generals of old would keep their troops together by stories of a weakened and scattered enemy. Such is the way of Satan for he would not dare let a sinner know the heart of the living God. Satan knows this would cause a revolution in his kingdom. Those poor sinners are drawn to the field of battle with a false concept of the Kingdom of Heaven. Then fairy tales and lies keep those poor souls there, wallowing in the death of guilt and shame. This is not the case with God. God through His word is not afraid to expose the Kingdom of Satan with all its supposed power.

We can instantly notice from this passage that we wrestle against four distinct elements of Satan's kingdom. What I find so interesting is the fact that Satan's kingdom is divided up and structured just like any other army in the world that you want to compare it to. For any army to be functional and effective they must have and operate smoothly four distinct elements. They are a command element, intelligence element, support element, and a combat element. Look again at the passage in Ephesians, we shall discover all four of those elements are listed and in that order. Let's break them down and talk about each element.

The first one mentioned is principalities, what is called the command element. The very word principality means a powerful ruler or commander. Notice how the word is listed in the plural sense. We know Satan is the ultimate commander and chief of this fallen kingdom. However this passage implies that we fight against many commanders under Satan's authority. Folks this isn't a play on words. Look at Daniel 10:13. Here we find an angel from Heaven answering Daniel's prayer and he tells Daniel that the prince of Persia held him up. He wasn't talking about an earthly prince, because it took Michael, one of the chief princes of God, to help overthrow the prince of Persia. Make no mistake this tells us that there was a particular principality over the area of Persia. Next notice in verse twenty of the same chapter of Daniel that the angel says there is another principality over the area of Grecia and after the prince of Persia is defeated this other prince will takeover the area of Persia as well as the area of Grecia. What we see is that every area in the world has a principality in charge of overseeing the will and operations of Satan.

We have no clear indication from scripture as to the breakdown of these principalities. In other words we really don't know if you have one per city, or state, etc... If you would be so kind as to allow me the freedom to draw upon my years of experience in dealing with the kingdom of Satan I will go so far as to say I believe there is one per county. My reasoning is this. In Daniel we see one principality over the whole area of Persia, and not just this town or that town in Persia. Also, if there had been more than one principality in the area of Persia than there would have been no need for the principality of Grecia to take over.

There is something else that jumps of the pages of this story in Daniel. It is clearly seen here that there is a strong sense of authority and rank structure in the kingdom of Satan. Take notice of the facts clearly stated in Daniel. First we see that the prince of Grecia did nothing to come and help the prince of Persia. Second the prince of Grecia had no authority over the area of Persia, and here we see that he did not overstep those bounds or his authority.

Most if not all command elements have no offensive weapons. I don't know too many commanders that carry M-16s, most carry maps and notes. That's why command central is never placed on the front lines; it stays well back of the friendly forces. This information becomes very useful later on down the road. Remember the Prince of Persia was defeated, and another principality took over.

The next element listed in Ephesians is the powers. Powers are what are called the intelligence element. You always find the powers listed right after the principalities. This is an interesting fact because in modern armies of today you always find the intelligence element closely following the command element. Vine's Expository Dictionary gives a good definition. It states the word powers comes "from the meaning of leave or permission, or liberty of doing as one pleases, the right to exercise power, or delegated influence."

One of the jobs I had in the Army was Counter Intelligence. We had certain freedoms, privileges and influence that other soldiers didn't have. I wasn't restricted to wearing a military uniform. I had freedom to move among any rank in the army. I was privileged to certain information that the other soldiers normally wouldn't see. I had some delegated influence through the information I presented to the commander. That information would help dictate the decisions he would make in battle.

The powers are the most deadly of the four elements for they are covert, and have the most influence on the command element. The powers as we shall see in the tactics chapter are able to wage war directly on the mind of man. Isaiah 24:21 says "the Lord will punish the powers in the heavens." It lists the powers by themselves here in Isaiah, for the purpose of punishment. As we shall see later the powers have both offensive and defensive weapons. They must be considered extremely hostile and dealt with accordingly.

The third element listed is the Rulers of the darkness of this world. The context of Ephesians 6:12, "not flesh and blood," implies they are not earthly rulers. These are spirit rulers, driven by the will of Satan under the permissive will of God, who exercise satanic authority over the world in its present condition of spiritual decay.

If you have rule or control over the world, then naturally you have access to its resources and supplies. That is why this is called the support element. If an army has no way to secure supplies, equipment, and resources, then that army cannot sustain itself. It is very obvious that the kingdom of Satan is very capable of recruiting people, and securing supplies to further its goals. We see this fact in the book of Job when the Sabians and the Chaldeans were used to attack Job.

The last element mentioned in Ephesians 6:12, is the spiritual wickedness in high places. To better understand what I call the combat element we need to understand the definition of spiritual wickedness. Spiritual means belonging to a spirit being that is higher than man but is inferior to God. Wickedness means evil desires or plots and purposes. The combat element of Satan's kingdom carries out the evil plots and desires of the principalities.

Spiritual wickedness is made up of fallen angels. Some humans can be recruited into this element by carrying out evil plots, purposes, and desires of the principalities. David, for example, was recruited in 1 Chronicles 21, when he allowed Satan to provoke him to number the troops of Israel. Even after his commanders of his army advised him not to do this foolish thing David still carried out the desire of the enemy. David was no more aware of being used by Satan than Peter was in Matthew 16:23. Even a man after God's own heart became spiritual wickedness in this instance.

William Gurnall once said this concerning the war between the kingdoms, "A war between the Saints and Satan, and that so bloody a one, that the cruelest which was ever fought by men will be found but sport and child's play to this." I, being a military veteran, have not seen nor heard of a conflict that has such intensity, and or casualties to show for the battle as the War between the Kingdoms.

3

Kingdom of Satan at Work

As we look at the kingdom of Satan in action, we must always remember it will never attack anyone or anything unless there is strategic value to be gained in the victory. Principalities will not waste resources to attack a fruitless target.

I found in the book of Job all four elements of Satan's kingdom at work and exposed for our viewing pleasure. I know most people read the book of Job and think poor Job. All we really see is POOR JOB! That's what I saw the first fourteen times I read it. After I had been studying spiritual warfare for some time, God kept bringing me back to the book of Job. I finally asked God why am I reading the book of Job again? It was then that what I am about to share with you became abundently clear to me. In fact it jumped off the pages at me. I couldn't believe I had missed that so many times before. Boy isn't the revelation of God good!

Let's look at this wonderful book together. We can see in the first chapter that there was a man named Job who lived in a town called Uz. I have heard of towns with bad names but this takes the cake. Can you imagine saying, "Hi, I am from Uzzzzz." Me neither, but that's another story. We find this man Job is one of upright character, who rebels against evil. Job had ten children and was protected and blessed by God.

In Job 1:6, we read that there is an appointed time that the angels came before the Lord. We gather from verse seven that the lord expected Satan to be there. The lord didn't say to Satan why are you here, or get out. The lord asked Satan where are you coming from today.

Listen to the answer given by Satan, "Then Satan answered the LORD, and said, from going to and fro in the earth, and from walking up and down in it." Satan only gave half the story didn't he? Satan's answer sounds familiar doesn't it. In 1 Pet. 5:8 we get the rest of the story: "Be sober, be vigilant; because your adversary the devil, as a roaring lion, walketh about, seeking whom he may devour." Notice he left out the fact that he was seeking someone to devour. However the Lord knows the rest of the story. Amen! What happens next should just blow you away.

"And the LORD said unto Satan, Hast thou considered my servant Job, that there is none like him in the earth, a perfect and an upright man, one that feareth God, and escheweth evil?" (Job 1:8 KJV). In essence the Lord turns to Satan and says, "Hey, have you considered my best soldier?" He goes on to say this guy is good, he is upright, and rebels against evil. What do you think about that Satan? When I first came to that understanding, I was taken back. I thought "man, I don't know if I want to be a great soldier if Jesus is going to expose me to the enemy." Then I had to laugh at myself, because I realized the Lord already knew Satan was seeking to devour Job. The Lord just beat him to the punch, and stated the obvious. Unlike in Daniel, here in the book of Job we find Satan himself assuming responsibility for the principality of Uz. Because Satan is commander of the fallen angels he must assume responsibility for all activity. When the Lord brings up this man called Job, Satan is under the watchful eye of the other sons of God and doesn't want to fail.

In Job 1:9-10, we see Satan starting to expose his kingdom for us. I want to write these scriptures out so we can glean all the meat from them that we can. "Then Satan answered the LORD, and said, Doth Job fear God for nought? Hast not thou made an hedge about him, and about his house, and about all that he hath on every side? thou hast blessed the work of his hands, and his substance is increased in the land"(KJV).

First consider the fact that Satan knows Job is protected on every side, and not just one side. He didn't say Job has a hedge on the east or west. No! Satan said about him, meaning all the way around him. How does someone know that you are protected on every side unless they attack you or recruit someone else to attack you? Also Satan knew Job was blessed and his substance was increasing. The only way to know someone's substance is increasing is to do a background investigation. You have to know what their substance was to begin with. The amount and rate of increase must also be determined. You can't have the sway of the whole world under your control and sit in one man's backyard. So we can safely say Satan wasn't doing the investigating of Job. In verse 10 we can already see the intelligence element (powers) raise its head.

The next bit of uncovering takes place in verses 13-15. Not only did the powers know Job's defenses and substance, but they also knew his very fears. No the powers didn't and can't read Job's mind. Job spoke his fears out loud. Look at verse 5 of chapter 1. Job was afraid his "sons and daughters had sinned and cursed God in their hearts." I believe the powers inserted that thought into Job's mind. You say how do I know that? Good question! First because the word of God tell us they can, "the devil having now put into the heart of Judas Iscariot, Simon's son, to betray him" (John 13:2 KJV). If that doesn't say enough just look at what Job said, "it may be that my son and daughters have sinned." Job didn't know of any particular sins they were committing. He for some reason assumed they might have sinned so he offered sacrifices daily for them. That reason was because the powers put that thought there.

Now look at verses 14 and 15. Take note of the first thing the kingdom of Satan went after. That's right his kids. The thing he feared most. What is ironic about this is the fact that the powers put the thoughts into Job's mind causing the fear. Then the first thing they went after was the very thing they caused.

In verse 15 we see the next element of Satan's kingdom exposed to the light. The rulers of the darkness (support element) recruited the Sabeans to attack Job's kids. The Sabeans attacked the servants tending the livestock around the house where the kids were. If the Sabeans were not in fact recruited, then why let someone live to tell Job? No! Only Satan wanted Job to know this information.

While that servant was telling Job about what happened, here came another servant. This servant tells of the combat element (spiritual wickedness), saying in verse 16, that fire came from heaven and burned up the sheep and servants. Again letting only one servant live to tell Job. We know God isn't raining fire on Job. This is from the "prince of the power of the air" (Eph. 2:1-3). Before that servant could finish along comes another servant.

This servant informs poor Job that His sons were killed when a great wind blew down the house. Look again at verse 18, "yet another messenger came and said, Your sons and daughters were feasting and drinking wine at the oldest brother's house." Do you see it? Job's daughters were in the house as well, yet they survived. Satan strategically targeted Job's most valuable possessions and assaulted his greatest fears. Sons of that day were valuable for they carried on the family name.

Can you imagine the thought process running through Job's mind? Job's probably thinking, the Sabeans took the livestock. Wow! That's close to the kids' house. Then fire from heaven, oh boy! That's getting even closer to the kids' house. Then the Chaldeans take more livestock and kill more servants. Oh no! That's on the other side of the kids' house. I am sure, as a father Job was ready to take off running towards the kids' house. I am sure he was anxious to see for himself what in the world was going on. He didn't get that chance because here comes another servant informing him of his loss.

What the casual observer to this tragic story first sees is POOR JOB! However I want you to shake that thought out of your head. We want to look past Job and see the real battle God exposed for you and me to witness and learn from. OK! Before you get all sappy saying, but what about poor Job? Let's see how this affected him. In verse 20 of chapter 1 we get our answer. "Then Job arose, and rent his mantle, and shaved his head, and fell down upon the ground, and worshipped" (KJV).

Notice the last word in that scripture, he worshipped God! You mean he didn't fall down on his knees and cry woe is me? You mean he didn't beg God to get his stuff back for him, crying why me? No! No! No! Job started praising God. Can you believe this guy! He fell down on his knees and lifted up the name of the Lord.

Now I know Job had some pretty bad feelings right about then, because he tore his clothes and shaved his head. I have had some pretty bad trials in my life, but I can't remember wanting to shave my head. Here we find Job not petitioning God for his needs, but instead praising God for what he had received. To the on-looker the outcome is not victory for the kingdom of Satan. God knew Job wouldn't curse Him. I believe Satan knew as well.

The question we must ask is why attack Job? Upon first glance there is no strategic value in this target called Job. Was it because God dangled Job in front of Satan like a carrot? We already saw in the first part of chapter 1, that Satan was consid-ering Job before he met with God. So I kept asking myself as I read the story of Job time and time again, what strategic value did Satan see? Then it hit me!

Look at how many people died in one day in that community. Think about this for a minute. Let's say for example, Bill Gates lived in your town. Who would you want to work for? Who would you want your kids to work for? That's right the one with the money. Well here we find Job the richest man in Uz. He, no doubt, had hundreds of servants and, because he was an honorable man, more than likely paid well. In one day how many children be-came fatherless? In one day how many parents are mourning the loss of a child? Who do you think all of those people are going to be mad at? Well, they are going to be mad at one of two people, Job or the Lord. They might even be mad at both.

Here is where I found the strategic value Satan was after. Job wasn't the target at all. He was the victim used to get to the target. The real target was the community of Uz. That is terrorist lesson 101. You attack the least number of people that will affect the great-est number of people. In the tactics chapter we will discuss this concept more fully.

Before we temporarily leave the book of Job, I want to show you spiritual wickedness in its true form. In chapter four of Job we read of a fallen angel speaking to Eliphaz one of Job's friends. I will shed some light on why this is a demon and not and angel from heaven. In verse 12, a thing was secretly brought to him and he only remembers a little of it. A point to consider is that no angel from God would talk to you without first calming you down. An angel of God would want you to remember everything not just a little. In verses 14–16 we see Eliphaz was terrified and a spirit passed before him but he could not tell what it looked like. Again, no angel of the Lord is going to let you stand there shaking in your pajamas. Not to mention that, every time an angel of the Lord appeared to someone, they could always tell its appearance. They would say; it's like the son of man, or a man clothed in white. Next in verse 17 and 18, we see this fallen angel tell half-truths and half-lies. In verse 17, he says man is not more just than God. That is true, however in verse 18, he says God puts no trust in his servants. That we know is a lie, or He wouldn't have trusted Moses, Noah, or Abraham. By these statements we can know that this was spiritual wickedness by way of a fallen angel carrying out the evil plots and schemes of the kingdom of Satan.

In the book of Job we find the kingdom of Satan at work. All of his elements are exposed for us to see their workings. I hope you have begun to learn a little of how the kingdom of Satan is setup and structured. We will go on from here and build upon what we have learned.

4

Kingdom of Heaven

What we have learned so far is that Satan's kingdom is an aggressive one. However the world doesn't rightfully belong to him. Due to the strongholds provided through the fall of man into sin, Satan has succeeded in gaining control. It is here that we find the scripture in 1 John 5:19 ringing true in our ears. "We know that we are children of God, and that the whole world is under the control of the evil one"(NIV).

Even though we have this bit of information we also know that the Kingdom of Heaven is the victorious kingdom, and that Christ according to Col. 2:10 has already won the war between the kingdoms. We know that Satan was the first aggressor in that he attacked the kingdom of heaven (Isa. 14:12–14). The good news is that when Jesus died on the cross and arose from the dead, he aggressively attacked the kingdom of Satan.

If you have one kingdom firmly in place and then another kingdom moves in on the first kingdom you are going to find yourself in a war. This is what we have in the world. Before the birth, death and resurrection of Jesus Christ the kingdom of Satan for the most part was not abated. That is why in the days of Noah, Satan dominated mankind with sin. Satan did this in order to stop the new king and new order that was coming.

Then along comes King Jesus. Even John the Baptist, when he saw Jesus said, "the kingdom of heaven is at hand" (Matt. 3:2). Jesus sent out his disciples, commanding them to preach the "gospel of the kingdom of heaven is at hand" (Matt. 10:7). Jesus preached the gospel of the kingdom (Matt. 4:23).

We miss the connection between the word gospel and its relations to the kingdom. When the word gospel is used in the New Testament it is overwhelmingly connected with King Jesus and His kingdom. So the gospel that we should take to the world today is the gospel of King Jesus and His kingdom of peace and love.

Here I must pause to share briefly the difference between the Kingdom of God, and the Kingdom of Heaven. The Kingdom of God is eternal. The Kingdom of Heaven is limited to Christ's Earthly reign both spiritual and millennial. Jesus was present in His Earthly ministry, to establish the Kingdom of Heaven in time and history. So while Jesus was with us the physical Kingdom of Heaven was at hand. Upon His ascension back to the Kingdom of God He established the church to be His spiritual Kingdom on Earth, in order to fight the spiritual battle against Satan's spiritual Kingdom. That is why Jesus sent the Holy Spirit to empower, equip, direct, and set forth the strategy for the churches battle against the forces of evil. I will share in great length about this concept in the "strategies" chapter.

Look at Matt. 24:14. "And this gospel of the kingdom will be preached in the whole world as a testimony to all nations, and then the end will come" (NIV). Jesus' mission while on Earth was to spread the good news (gospel) of the Kingdom of Heaven. Jesus showed us what the Kingdom is like. He even showed us the entrance to the Kingdom. When we think of the word kingdom we think of a king. In order to have a kingdom you must have a reigning king. The king that is reigning over the Kingdom of Heaven is King Jesus.

I have talked a lot about the Kingdom of Heaven. This would be a good time to look at what is meant by the gospel of that Kingdom. Most people associate the word gospel with salvation. However salvation is but the entrance to the kingdom. The word gospel means good news. Oh what good news it is. We have this New Kingdom with its laws and principles, which supersede the laws and principles of the Kingdom of Satan. As pertaining to salvation, we can say the gospel is the ark of the New Testament, where Noah was the Old Testament ark. Paul tells us: "when once the long suffering of God waited in the days of Noah, while the ark was a preparing, wherein few, that is, eight souls were saved by water. The like figure whereunto even baptism doth also now save us by the resurrection of Jesus Christ: Who is gone into heaven, and is on the right hand of God; angels and authorities and powers being made subject unto him" (KJV). God saved Noah out of the corrupt world system by way of the ark. In like manner, God saved us out of the sinful world system by way of the good news of the Kingdom of Jesus Christ (gospel).

Salvation is not all-inclusive to the word gospel. Salvation is the good news towards man through Christ. On the other hand the gospel of the Kingdom is also good news towards God through Christ.

The gospel is a kingdom message and we, as Christians, need to understand how the laws and principles of the kingdom of Christ operate in order to maintain our daily victory. The church should be an equipping center for Christians, instead we have become a salvation center. Now I am not saying salvation is wrong. On the contrary we should be taking Christ into the world. Then bringing them into the church to be trained in the laws and principles that govern the Kingdom they have enlisted in. Let me make it very clear I do not despise the preaching of salvation. But if all of our works are limited to the winning of souls through salvation, and we don't go on in training of those souls, then Satan has not been administered a fatal blow. If we fail to regain the world from the hand of Satan, then we have failed to arrive at God's original purpose for introducing the Kingdom of Heaven to man. If all our efforts are redemptive of man alone, then we fail to redeem the world back to the Kingdom of Heaven.

Think about what it would take to become a citizen of any country. You would have to know the laws and principles that govern that country. You would have to swear allegiance to that country. You would also have to swear to defend that country. It is no different in the Kingdom of heaven. We must know the laws and principles that govern our New Kingdom. We swear allegiance to the King. We also swear to defend the Kingdom truths. Salvation is the port of entry, where we have undertaken the swearing in of our citizenship into the Kingdom of heaven. Keep in mind, beloved, that we have been saved out of our old corrupt kingdom, and into the New Kingdom of Jesus Christ. We can't take up residency at the port of entry. We must move on through faith into the freedom of our New Kingdom.

Now let's share a little about what is the Kingdom of Heaven. It is interesting how God has set most things up in a trinity. You have the trinity of God, the trinity of man, and the trinity of the universe. We also find the Kingdom of Heaven divided up into a trinity. It has a social, economic, and governmental part. In fact both man's kingdom and Satan's kingdom are set up the same way. Let's look at the three parts.

The Kingdom of Heaven's social system is one of unselfishness, full of compassion and forgiveness, composed of love, desiring to build up one another. Man's social system, which Satan's kingdom utilizes, is the complete opposite. It is a selfish one, filled with manipulation and hate, desiring to tear others down in order to build themself up. People say wait the world has wonderful social programs to help the needy and poor. However an honest observer can see that those programs have been used more to keep the poor in that condition than really help them out.

Let's look at the second part of the trinity. The Kingdom of Heaven's economic system is one of sacrificial giving. Which, again is in complete contrast to the world's economic system of hoarding and selfish gain and always wanting more.

On to the third part of the trinity, which is the Kingdom of Heaven's governmental system. We find it is one of servanthood. Never wanting recognition or vainglory but only wanting the King to be see in the best light. On the other hand as can clearly be seen in the last elections, man's governmental system is all about self- serving power. Praise be to God through the blood of Jesus Christ, we can now say to Satan's kingdom the party is over, because the "Son of God was manifested, that he might destroy the works of the devil"(1 John 3:8). No longer, brothers and sisters, are we bound by the Old Kingdom but are risen into the New Kingdom. Let us continually pursue the New Kingdom laws and principles.

5

Base of Operation

Unfortunately Satan hasn't conceded his defeat. He is continually trying to overthrow the Kingdom of Heaven. Keeping this in mind, all Christians must remember that we have enlisted in a kingdom that is at war. To totally expose Satan to you without giving you the much needed information on how to defeat that kingdom is dangerous indeed. You have heard the old saying about having "just enough information to be dangerous." I don't want us to fall into that category. I desire us to have the fullness of knowledge, so that we can be successful in the kingdom of Christ.

Every good soldier has a base of operation. It is no different in the Kingdom of Heaven. In order to fight the good fight we must understand our base of operation given by God, through Christ, and maintained by the Holy Spirit. This base of operation is the tabernacle or what is known as the temple. In the New Testament we are told quite frequently that our body is the temple of a living God (1 Cor. 3:16-17; 6:19-20, 2 Cor. 6:16). The New Testament goes on to say that our temple is bought with a price and we should glorify God in that temple. I found that only when we operate the temple in the way the Kingdom of Heaven has prescribed can we find lasting success in the kingdom.

The question is do we really know how to accomplish this task? I can testify in my own life there was a time I didn't know how. I thought: "you know what I need? I need a representative of the temple to give me a working tour—a 'minister of the sanctuary' that can explain how it all works." If you've ever tried to find a representative lately they are rare indeed. But praise be to God, for we find in Hebrews 8:1, that He supplied one for us in a King Jesus. "Now of the things which we have spoken this is the sum: We have such an high priest, who is set on the right hand of the throne of the Majesty in the heavens; a minister of the sanctuary, and of the true tabernacle, which the Lord pitched, and not man" (Hebrews 8:1–2 KJV). Jesus is that minister through the tour guide of the Holy Spirit that brings us into the fullness of understanding.

The book of Hebrews is considered the book of comparisons. Paul compares the old Mosaic tabernacle to the new tabernacle. He compares the old covenant to the new covenant. He compares the old law to the new law. Here in chapter 8 Paul tells us that of everything that he has said up to this point, this is the sum or completion. In order to understand the sum or completion of what Paul is telling us there is some background information that we need to know. To fully understand our base of operation it is imperative that we grasp some of these concepts Paul is mentioning here in Hebrews.

So bear with me as we go through this part. I won't list them here, but I would suggest that you go back and read chapters 6 and 7 of Hebrews. I will be sharing some thoughts from those chapters that are important to the subject at hand. In chapters 6 and 7 Paul compares Jesus to the king-priest of Salem called Melchisedec. Melchisedec was a Gentile king who was recognized as a priest by Abraham. Because he was a Gentile king he had no recorded birth, mother, father, or death. Melchisedic was a type of Jesus since he had no recorded beginning or end. Likewise Jesus is the beginning and the end. He is the Alpha and Omega. Paul takes great lengths to show the greatness of the priesthood under Melchisedic. Then Paul lets down the boom. He says that if this great, wonderful, Levitical priesthood (whereby the law was given) were perfect, there would have been no need for another priest like Melchisedic to come along. What Paul is telling us is that since the priesthood was not perfect there was a need for a more perfect priesthood after the order of God. He goes on to say, since the priesthood is changing it is necessary that the law change as well.

Then we come to chapter 8 where Paul informs us that the old priesthood and old law, and the old tabernacle was just a shadow

or an example of the perfect priesthood in Christ, and the perfect
law that His ministry brings to the new tabernacle. Let's look at
some of the scriptures that confirm this for us:

> For if he were on earth, he should not be a priest,
> seeing that there are priests that offer gifts
> according to the law: Who serve unto the example
> and shadow of heavenly things. Heb. 8:4–5 (KJV)

> The Holy Ghost this signifying, that the way into
> the holiest of all was not yet made manifest, while
> as the first tabernacle was yet standing: which was
> a figure for the time then present. Heb. 9:8–9
> (KJV)

> For the law having a shadow of good things to
> come, and not the very image of the things, can
> never with those sacrifices, which they offered year
> by year continually, make the comers thereunto
> perfect. Heb. 10:1 (KJV)

Paul states over and over again that these are just the shadow
and not the very image of the true. That's why in verses 20–22 of
chapter 7, Paul tells us that the old was not given by an oath. He
goes on to say that the new is given by an oath. If you were called
to court to testify of a crime you witnessed, but the only thing you
saw was a shadow and not the very person committing the crime.
Would you have a good testimony? Well no! You can't testify of a
shadow. Likewise God didn't make an oath pertaining to the
shadow. God made an oath with the one casting the shadow. Paul
continues by saying that this oath makes Jesus the mediator of a
better covenant (Heb. 7:22; 8:6; 9:15). We could spend three pages
stating the eighty-five differences between the old covenant and
the new covenant, but I will just share a few here:

- The old came by way of Moses the new came by
  way of Christ.

- The old was the law of sin the new is the law of righteousness.

- The old brought death the new brings life.

- The old ended by Christ the new started by Christ.

We could go on and on with examples, but I am sure you see my point.

Before we dive into the new tabernacle let's look at the shadow as represented by the old tabernacle.

THE OLD TABERNACLE

Look at Hebrews 8:5. "Who serve unto the example and shadow of heavenly things, as Moses was admonished of God when he was about to make the tabernacle: for, See, saith he, that thou make all things according to the pattern shewed to thee in the mount"(KJV). I want us to look closely at two words Paul is telling us that were spoken to Moses by God. The first word is admonished. The word admonished means warned. So we see God waning Moses to build the tabernacle according to a pattern.

Most people think that God told Moses how to build the tabernacle and he just remembered all the details and went out and built it. According to the next word I want us to examine, that wasn't the case. The word pattern comes from the Greek word *tupos,* which means a die or model of resemblance. In Exodus 25 we see the Hebrew word for pattern called *tabnit. Tabnit* is translated structure, figure, form or likeness. *Tabnit* is associated with another word—*banah,* which means to build a house, and also refers to the act of raising children. In the Bible a house may often referred to a family. That is why in Ruth chapter 4, we see the wives of Jacob (Rachel and Leah) are called the builders of the *tabnit* or house of Israel. By this we can see how *tupos* and *tabnit* relate to the house of God and human form.

What we see in Exodus 25 is that God literally gave Moses a physical model of the tabernacle and all the instruments that went into that tabernacle (Exodus 25:9). Then from verse 10 through verse 39, God sets out to describe the material that will be used to build the tabernacle and all the instruments. In verse 40 Moses is warned again to make sure he builds the tabernacle after the model that he was given.

Why was God so adamant about the building of this tabernacle? Remember this was to be a shadow of good things to come (Heb. 10:1). Everything about this tabernacle from the construction layout to the way it operated was a shadow, and had to be a perfect representation of the true image casting that shadow.

King David passed down to Solomon the same literal model that was given to Moses by God. I ran across a research article on the Internet written by Tony Badillo who was a temple researcher. The article was entitled, "King Solomon's Temple Secrets." In this article he talks about the appearance of a human form in the layout of the temple structure and instruments in the temple. Mr. Badillo's article makes for a good argument for the temple being "fashioned after the likeness of three biblical figures, a Temple Man, Jacob, and a Metallic Messiah." He goes on to share that "all three appear in a single composition, with one figure imposed atop the other." For our discussion we will only look at the Temple Man and how it relates to the topic at hand. However you might want to visit Mr. Badillo's web site (**http://home.earthlink.net/ ~tonybadillo**) for the complete article. I think you will find it a most rewarding study.

Paul told us in Hebrew 8:6 that Jesus is the minister of the true tabernacle, and that He is the first true tabernacle that is casting the shadow. The fact that Solomon's temple was constructed in the form of a high priest is significant indeed. We already discovered that Jesus is a high priest above all others. We also know that all the objects or instruments in the temple refer to Jesus. Jesus said in John 8:12, "I am the light of the world which relates to the lamps in the Holy Place. In John 6:35 Jesus said, "I am the bread of Life, which relates to the bread on the "tables of the showbread." We could go on and show how everything in the temple relates to Jesus, but that is not our aim here in this book. There are plenty of good books on that topic so I will not take up space here to share those thought. We shall see later how after the new birth we become the true tabernacles that cast the shadow.

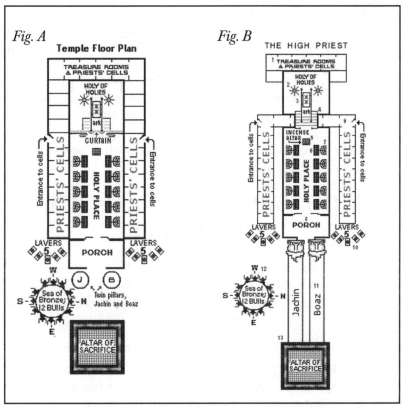

Illustrations courtesy of Tony Badillo, "King Solomon's Temple Secrets"

A picture, they say, is worth a thousand words. Mr. Badillo has some of the best illustrations of the shadow concept so let us look at some of these in hopes to gain a better understanding of what I am saying.

On the left (Fig. A), you see the original floor plan. On the right (Fig. B), you see the floor plan transformed into the figure of a high priest. At the top, the priests' cells form the high priest's turban. Then the Holy of Holies forms the head. The two large stars making up the eyes are the Cherubs of gold- plated olivewood. The Ark of the Covenant with its poles is the nose. On the North and South sides, more priests' cells form the arms. The onyx stones that were worn on the left and right shoulders of the high priest correspond to the north and south entrances. The staircase leading up to the Holy of

Holies makes up the neck and throat. The Holy place makes up the main body. The porch makes the hips and pelvis. The two pillars of Jachin and Boaz when laid down make the legs of the Temple Man. The five bronze Lavers on each side of the porch form the ten fingers of the hands. The Altar of Sacrifice makes the feet of the Temple Man. We can see how this is a shadow of the new temple. That new temple is man as we shall come to understand in its fullness later. Now maybe we can grasp an understanding of why God was so unbending on the fact that Moses was to follow the pattern he was given. It had to be a perfect shadow.

THE CONSTRUCTION LAYOUT OF THE TEMPLE

Not only was the construction layout to be a shadow, but the daily operation and function of the temple was also to be a shadow of the new temple. Let's view those scriptures that bring this to light for us:

> In whom all the building fitly framed together groweth unto an holy temple in the Lord: In whom ye also are builded together for an habitation of God through the Spirit.
> Eph 2:21–22 (KJV)

> And what agreement hath the temple of God with idols? for ye are the temple of the living God; as God hath said, I will dwell in them, and walk in them; and I will be their God, and they shall be my people. 2 Cor 6:16 (KJV)

> Do you not know that your body is a temple of the Holy Spirit, who is in you, whom you have received from God? You are not your own; you were bought at a price. Therefore honor God with your body. 1 Cor 6:19–20 (NIV)

> Know ye not that ye are the temple of God, and
> that the Spirit of God dwelleth in you? 1 Cor 3:16
> (KJV)

We know that the old Temple was made in three parts. Again we see the trinity at work. There was an outer court, an inner court, and the Holy of Holies. This is a perfect shadow of man. Listen to what 1 Thess. 5:23, has to say about the trinity of man. "And the very God of peace sanctify you wholly; and I pray God your whole spirit and soul and body be preserved blameless unto the coming of our Lord Jesus Christ" (KJV). From this we understand that we are made in three parts just like the Old Temple.

We have an outer court called flesh. We have an inner court called the soul. We have a Holy of Holies called the spirit.

DAILY OPERATIONS OF THE TEMPLE

OUTER COURT

In the old Temple, the one made with hands, the first thing you would notice would be the outer court. In Moses' temple a fence of white linen enclosed the outer court. The fence represented Jesus as the mediator between God and man (1 Tim. 2:5). A mediator is one who accepts an official position between two parties. The outside world recognized the temple of God by way of this outer court. It brought world awareness to the temple. It is through the physical body, called flesh, that we come into contact with the material world. So we can say the corporal body gives us world consciousness. Through the flesh man is in contact with the outside sensuous world, affecting if and being affected by it. Just like the old Temple, we are recognized by way of the outer court. People know us by the clothes we wear, by our mannerisms, our hairstyle, and even our voice. Our senses and feelings as well as our outward actions come from the body. As God purifies the flesh through the Spirit, we become the white linen fence that mediates between the lost and Jesus Christ.

We are told that the first Temple had divine ordinances and services that had to be performed (Heb. 9:1). The new Temple also has divine ordinances and services that must be performed. The first thing you would notice upon entering the old Temple would be the large brazen altar. It was here that you had to lay down a sacrifice. You could wander around all day in the court-yard never receiving the instructions of God until you laid down a sacrifice. You could never proceed to the Holy place, what was also called the decision-making place as well as many other names without giving the sacrifice. To move past the outer court some-thing had to die. That was a divine ordinance that had to be ful-filled in order to proceed on. In the new Temple we find this same brazen altar in the outer court called self. We can wander around in our feelings all day. We can gratify our senses all day. As long as we feed the fatted calf of our feelings and senses; refusing to lay them down on the altar we will never proceed to the Holy place. Paul states it this way, "I beseech you therefore, brethren, by the mercies of God, that ye present your bodies a living sacrifice, holy, acceptable unto God, which is your reasonable service" (Rom. 12:1 KJV). This, my brothers and sisters is the divine ser-vice of our new Temple. We must die to our feelings and emo-tions. No longer can we afford to be driven by our feelings and emotions. The Spirit of a Holy God must drive us.

In order for that to happen we must not wander aimlessly around in the outer court of self, but quickly run to the altar and die to self. I cannot stress this point enough. For as Romans 8:13 tells us if you live or pursue after your feelings and emotions you will die. However, if through the power of the spirit you mortify those feelings and emotions of the flesh you will live. The seed God has planted in you through faith in Jesus Christ cannot come to life unless you die to self (1 Cor. 15:36). You are the first benefi-ciary of your own death. Wow! What a great benefit plan. Amen! There isn't a 401K made today that can top God's benefit pack-age! Think about this for a minute. If the self- part of me (feelings and emotions) dies, then the insurance or benefit plan kicks in and cuts a check to the beneficiaries of the deceased. The beauty of this plan is that I am the beneficiary. My spirit is still alive to accept and cash that check. Look at the following scriptures that tell of the benefit plan. "I am crucified with Christ: nevertheless I live; yet not I, but Christ liveth in me: and the life which I now live in the flesh I live by the faith of the Son of God, who loved me, and gave himself for me" (Gal. 2:20 KJV). "And if Christ be in you, the body is dead because of sin; but the Spirit is life because of righteousness" (Rom. 8:10 KJV). "Likewise reckon ye also yourselves to be dead indeed unto sin, but alive unto God through Jesus Christ our Lord" (Rom. 6:11 KJV).

As you die to self (feelings and emotions) you can live to Christ. You will come to understand how to accomplish this more completely a few pages down the road, but for now know this. The keys to dying to yourself are this DO NOT TAKE ANYTHING PERSONALLY!

The minute you take things personally, those things, no matter what they are, become a conflict. A conflict can never be won, only managed. Let me give you a practical example of what I am talking about. There was a young married couple. It was rapidly approaching their second anniversary and the husband wanted to get his wife a very special gift. However, since they were newly married they didn't have a lot of money. The husband decided to work overtime for a whole month in order to afford her present. The wife being six months pregnant was feeling fat and ugly. Her self-esteem was dipping a little bit. The powers (intelligence element) thought this would be a great opportunity to interject their thoughts into her mind. It sounds something like this: "why is hubby working so late? Maybe he doesn't find me attractive anymore! You know that new secretary down there at his office sure is pretty!"

Do you see what's happening? The powers are trying to get her to accept these thoughts as her own. You see this is just a problem it's not personal yet. If the powers stop here she more than likely can fight them off by talking to her husband. That conversation might sound like this: "Honey why have you been working so hard lately? Are you trying to stay away from your fat, pregnant wife?" We know he loves his wife. That is why he is working to get a present. So more than likely he would confirm his love for her and make her feel better. The powers are not so foolish to stop there though, because it's not personal to her yet. So they would continue the assault, by pushing more thoughts. Those thoughts might be: "he's probably having an affair. He can't treat you this way! You cook and clean for him. Who does he think he is anyway?" Do you see the difference? Now it's personal. No longer is it a problem to be solved. No! It is a conflict to be managed. When the husband comes home she is going to let him have it. No longer talking to him from love, but out of anger. She will tell him: "who do you think you are coming in here late again? You've been out shacking up with the new secretary haven't you? What, I am good enough to get pregnant but not good enough to come home to." I know you are probably thinking, boy sounds like he is speaking from experience. Well no, even though I have had my share of conflicts this isn't my past. It comes from a couple that I counseled years ago. You get the point nonetheless. As soon as she took those thoughts personally the situation became a conflict.

Men you are not off the hook. As soon as she railed on him the powers moved in on him for the kill. He then received the thought: "here I have been working my head off for her and this is the way she treats me." Now we have a fight on our hands. At any point either one, husband or wife could have died to their feelings and emotions and stopped this conflict. If they don't then the relationship will die. Rom. 8:13 is true, there will be a sacrifice or a death. Either way something is going to die, by choice or providence. When we do not die to ourselves and wander around in the outer court this is what the Bible calls natural man, which is an individual controlled by the lust of the flesh.

Think for a moment about Abraham as he laid Isaac on the altar. Here this father was about to take his most loved and kill him, that being his son. Abraham was taking the thing closest and dearest to his heart and laying it on the altar. That, my brothers and sisters, is what we do when we die to self. We take those sins closest and dearest to our hearts; those fleshly desires that have promised the greatest return of pleasure and lay them on the altar. Can you now feel with some surety the feelings and emotions of Abraham at the altar looking down at Isaac. The only difference is the lust of the flesh will not lie so quietly on the altar, as did Isaac.

This is why so many Christians run the race, but so few obtain the prize. This is why we find so many Christians who take up position on the battlefield of life, but few come out as victors on the other side of that field.

This is why we must remember that in the outer court man is identified with the death of Jesus. "Knowing this, that our old man is crucified with him, that the body of sin might be destroyed, that henceforth we should not serve sin. For he that is dead is freed from sin" (Rom. 6:6–7 KJV). Remember in the garden of Gethsemane Jesus prayed to God "let this cup pass from me." The cup of separation was what Jesus wanted to pass from Him. Think about this, Jesus God in the flesh had never been separated from the mind of the Father. Always Jesus knew the directive and heard the instruction given. Never had Jesus been separated from the life giving force of the Holy Spirit. Now upon taking on the whole world's sin, he was being separated. Can you imagine the feelings and emotions running through Jesus? No wonder He cried out: "Father, if I could go to the cross without being separated from you let it be." "Father, if I can fulfill your plan without separation please let it be." But there was no other way. Jesus had to die to self in order for us to be identified with His death. Make no mistake, if we are to be identified with His death of self, how much more are we to be identified with His resurrection unto life.

This reminds me of a *Star Trek* episode where the good guys were fighting an enemy called the Borg. Now the Borg was a group of drones that acted as one called The Collective. Their whole purpose for existence was to assimilate anyone and anything they came into contact with. The Borg's main saying was "you will be assimilated, resistance is futile!" That's the way Satan's kingdom is. They are a huge collective roaming around assimilating people. They scream resistance is futile. But our identification with Jesus Christ through His death cries resistance is profitable unto life.

What happens when we fail to resist the flesh and self? The body beats the soul into submission. The soul drags the spirit kicking and screaming into sin. Let me show you what this looks like in hopes that you can readily see the problem and fix it. Situations come up in our lives, which causes feelings. The feelings cause emotions, which sparks thoughts. Those thoughts provoke us to action. Our action brings reaction or what is called consequences. The consequences bring more feelings, which bring more emotion and so on and so forth.

You get the idea; there we find a vicious circle that brings an emotional roller coaster of a life. When that situation comes up we must make a conscious effort to not respond to those feelings. If we don't they will stir worldly emotions. Those worldly emotions will spark carnal emotional thought called sin (anger, malice, hate, vengeance, and lust). Then the carnal thought creates a worldly action called sins. Only when we make a conscious effort to ignore those feelings and emotions can we proceed to the Holy place of decision.

THE SANCTUARY

"Likewise reckon ye also yourselves to be dead indeed unto sin, but alive unto God through Jesus Christ our Lord. Let not sin therefore reign in your mortal body, that ye should obey it in the lusts thereof. Neither yield ye your members as instruments of unrighteousness unto sin: but yield yourselves unto God, as those that are alive from the dead, and your members as instruments of righteousness unto God" (Rom. 6:11–13 KJV).

Jesus knows how difficult this is for us, and wants to help us. Notice He is not asking us to do anything He hasn't already done Himself. Remember we are crucified with Him. The minute you ignore those feelings, laying them down on the altar something wonderful happens. Just like in the Old Temple you would proceed through the veil into the Holy place (decision-making place). It is here that the priest dwelt, daily ministering to the people. Our decision-making place is called the soul or mind of man. The soul stands between the body and the spirit, binding these two together. The spirit can control the body by way of the medium of the soul. Also the body can by way of the soul make man's spirit love the world. The soul makes it possible for the spirit and body to communicate and cooperate. The soul gives us self-consciousness, because our will, emotions, and intellect all come from the soul. Our volition or will comes from the soul (Ps 27:12; 35:25; Ezek. 16:27; Deut. 21:14). Our intellect, reasoning, understanding, in effect, our mind comes from the soul (Prov. 19:2; 3:21-22; Ps 139:14). We see from these scriptures that man's knowledge exists through the soul. Our emotions comes from the soul (Song of Sol. 1:7; 2 Sam. 5:8; Zech. 11:8; Deut. 14:26; Ezek. 24:21; Isa. 61:10).

The reason Paul in Hebrews takes the time to show why Jesus' Priesthood was so much greater than all others is because of our soul. Read carefully what Paul tells us in Heb. 8:2. "A minister of the sanctuary, and of the true tabernacle, which the Lord pitched, and not man" (KJV). Jesus is the minister (priest) of our sanctuary called the soul. If you remember the sanctuary is also called the decision-making place. We make our decisions in our mind called the soul. How does Jesus minister to our soul? Well, we know from John 1:1 that "In the beginning was the Word, and the Word was with God, and the Word was God."

Right off the bat we know that God's written word is going to minister to our soul. How does it do this? By renewing our minds through knowledge. "And have put on the new man, which is renewed in knowledge after the image of him that created him:" (Col. 3:10 KJV). We are starting to see another key before us. Let me see if I can brush away the cobwebs and expose fully this key. Look at John 14:26. "But the Comforter, which is the Holy Ghost, whom the Father will send in my name, he shall teach you all things, and bring all things to your remembrance, whatsoever I have said unto you" (KJV). The Holy Spirit, which God gave us through the blood of Jesus, wants to renew a right thinking in us. He does this by bringing the word of God back to our remembrance. The Holy Spirit cannot call to remembrance what we haven't put in our mind to begin with. There is the fullness of that key. You must know the word of God.

OK, let's break this down and show its practical application. What does this look like in action? The minute you ignore the feelings of the flesh, Jesus through His word by way of the Holy Spirit will bring that word to the front of your mind. There you find yourself standing in the decision-making place (Sanctuary). There you must make a decision. Do I accept the Lordship of Jesus Christ or do I accept the lordship of the flesh and this world? This happens in a split second. This isn't drug out over a period of time. Here let me give you an example. There is this young teenage boy walking down the road. He sees laying in the road a pornographic magazine. Now his flesh wants him to pick it up and look, but his spirit convicts his conscience to walk past and not look. Let's say for now that the boy ignored his feelings in essence dies to himself. The minute he walks past the book. The very first step past that book the Holy Spirit floods His mind with the words of God! Remembering greater is He that is in me than he that is in the world, and scripture after scripture about how lust would destroy him. Let's say the boy didn't die to himself but picked up the magazine and looked. The minute he chose the lordship of self, the Spirit is going to convict him with guilt and shame. At that moment a piece of that boy will die. The old adage pay now or pay later comes to mind. You can pay now and chose to die, or pay later and a piece of you dies, but sooner or later death will come. You can bow before Jesus now by choosing to die to self or you can bow later when death is not an option. Take note how important knowing the word of God is. If the boy didn't have the word of God in the files of his soul, then there would be nothing for the Holy Spirit to convict him of.

Romans 12:2 tells us that we are not to be conformed to our flesh but transformed by the renewing power of the Holy Spirit in our mind. Then we can show what is the perfect will of God. Have you noticed that everything depends on you knowing the word of God? Why is this so important?

God knows that the battle lines of the war between the kingdoms have been drawn in the sand of your mind. Our brain is like a big supercomputer. When information is obtained it is separated, categorized, and placed in files called memories. When the word dog is mentioned, for example, one person might call to remembrance the loving pet they had as a child. However, somebody else might remember the horror of the dog that attacked him or her as a child. The same file sparked emotions of joy for one and fear for the other.

The brain, like a computer, when asked a question will search all the files that pertain to that question and give an answer based on the information contained in those files. How we ask the question will determine the answer given. If you were working on a math program in the computer you wouldn't ask an English question, because you wouldn't get an answer. English isn't found in a math program. It is said that we hold a conversation with ourselves at over three hundred words per minute.

We are constantly asking ourselves questions. If we pose those questions in a negative way the brain is going to search all the applicable negative files for the answer. For example, I have heard ladies say, why can't I lose weight? Or why can't I keep weight off? The word can't triggers the brain to search all the negative files, and for some of us that's a lot of files. The answer that comes back to us might sound like this. That's the way I was born! I can't exercise, it hurts my back! I can't change. Using our example above if we asked the same question in a positive way we would get a positive answer. If we said how can I lose weight and enjoy it? Then the brain would search all the positive files and find an answer equally positive.

Most Christians do not have the positive words of God in their memory bank. It is very difficult for the Holy Spirit to call to our remembrance what is not there to begin with. That's like drawing money on an empty checking account. You are going to come up short every time. The battle is going to be won or lost in your soul. We read this truth in 2 Cor. 10:3-6. "For though we walk in the flesh, we do not war after the flesh: (For the weapons of our warfare are not carnal, but mighty through God to the pulling down of strong holds;) Casting down imaginations, and every high thing that exalteth itself against the knowledge of God, and bringing into captivity every thought to the obedience of Christ; And having in a readiness to revenge all disobedience, when your obedience is fulfilled"(KJV).

Listen to what it says. Our fight isn't in the flesh because we are supposed to be dead to our flesh. I don't know of any good dead fighters. Our weapons can't be carnal because dead men carry no weapons. This scripture is very clear as to where the battle is raging. Where are the vain imaginations lurking to attack us? In our mind! Where are the intellectual thoughts that are pushing against the knowledge of the word of God? In our mind! Where are the thoughts hiding in the darkness waiting to be drug into captivity? In our mind! The radio, TV, books, and magazines all want to spoil your memory banks. Even religious traditions of men and the rudiments of the world want to corrupt your program, destroying your files (Col. 2:8).

Before we were regenerated by the new birth of salvation, we walked according to the ways of our flesh and this world (Eph. 2:1). Let me paint this picture for you. Before salvation the powers (intelligence element) had taken up residence in your mind (soul). They were kicked back with the remote control in hand, sipping iced tea. They were comfortable, welcomed soul owners. Then their dwelling place got sold. That's right it was bought with a price, and that being the blood of Jesus. So the eviction notice was sent out. There isn't enough room for the Holy Spirit and evil spirits in the same house. You can't serve the master of self and King Jesus at the same time. So Satan, self and the world come home to find the locks have been changed and their stuff is in the yard.

Here is where the trouble starts! You see our flesh owes a debt to sin and death that we cannot pay. As long as you wander around in the outer court of self then Satan, self, and the world will chase you down, demanding payment, which is rightfully due them. This is where most Christians live today. With self, Satan, and the world banging on the doors and windows screaming "let me in, let me in!" Listen carefully brothers and sisters to what you are about to read! You cannot get payment from a dead man, for dead men owe no debts. Did you get that? If you die to self, those feelings and emotions we talked about, then the debt has been paid. The blood of Jesus is the receipt of the payment in full. So now we have the minister of the sanctuary moving in. He is going to bring with Him all of His furnishings. The furnishing He brings is the word of God. Through the new tenant of our soul we can begin to put on the new man, which is after the image of Jesus Christ.

THE HOLY OF HOLIES

After laying down self upon the brazen altar in the outer court, we found ourselves standing in the holy place before the presence of the minister of the sanctuary, King Jesus. Once we heard and obeyed the word of God, and accepted the Lordship of Jesus Christ we began to feel the blessing of the Holy Spirit of God in the Holy of Holies.

Of the three elements that make up the trinity of man the spirit is the most virtuous for it possess the ability to join with God by way of the Holy Spirit. Due to this fact we can say that the spirit gives us God consciousness. At the new birth we receive the Holy Spirit, but this should not be confused with our spirit for they are not one and the same. If we cannot discern our own spirit, how will we be able to commune with the Spirit of God? If we cannot discern our spirit, then we will easily make the mistake of substituting the thoughts of the mind (soul) for the words of the spirit. That could force us to wander around in the outer court. Let me list just a few scripture here that show us that we have a spirit separate from that of the Holy Spirit: 1 Cor. 2:11; 5:4; 14:14; 14:32; Heb. 12:23; Prov. 25:28.

We as Christians must acknowledge the fact that we have a spirit, something extra to the soul, which is to say our thoughts, imaginations, and intellect. The spirit of man is beyond the sensations of the flesh. Thanks to Adam man is a fallen creature. When God told Adam "you shall surely die," He was talking about man's spirit. We see this example in the fall of Satan. Satan is a spiritual creature designed to live forever. However when he fell he broke communion with God. Now this fallen angel has no virtue of Godliness to be found in him. Can we then say Satan no longer exists? We know that is not the case. Satan's condition only separated his relationship with God. Man is no different, once sin entered man, the relationship our spirit enjoyed with the Holy Spirit was severed. At that moment did man's spirit cease to exist? The answer would be no! No more than Satan's did upon his fall. Though man's spirit still exists, it did, however, plunge into darkness unable to rule the trinity of man in the manner it had before the fall. No religious tradition of man, no Earthly enlightenment or law can restore the condition of man's spirit. Man without God is forevermore a man of the flesh. In order to reach above our fallen state, in order to go back in time as it where, and get back what man had before the fall; the spirit must be regenerated. Only God, through the blood of Jesus Christ, by way of the restoring power of the Holy Spirit, can make man anew. The rebirth of a sinner occurs first in his spirit. God's redemptive work always begins within the center of man, and then works outward towards the flesh. As we shall see in the tactics portion of the book, Satan works in the opposite manner. Satan's kingdom always goes after the weakest part being the flesh, and then works inward towards man's spirit. Now you see why the battle lines are drawn in man's soul. For you now see this is where the two kingdoms collide: God is working from within man and Satan is working from the outside.

Upon reading John 3:6, we see that the new birth comes the moment God's Holy Spirit touches our dead spirit, "that which is born of the flesh is flesh; and that which is born of the Spirit is spirit" (KJV). This new regenerated spirit cannot sin according to 1 John 3:9. "Whosoever is born of God doth not commit sin; for his seed remaineth in him: and he cannot sin, because he is born of God" (KJV). Despite this fact listen to what 2 Cor 7:1 tells us. "Having therefore these promises, dearly beloved, let us cleanse ourselves from all filthiness of the flesh and spirit, perfecting holiness in the fear of God" (KJV). It appears that our spirit of new birth can be and often times is defiled. Think about this for just a moment. We are given something I don't believe Adam was privy to. Not only did God resurrect our dead spirit through new birth, but in addition gave us a new spirit of life in Christ Jesus. Let's look at each part that makes up the trinity of man's spirit.

From scripture we can learn that our spirit, that is to say our human spirit, is made up of three parts. Here again we see in the spirit the concept of the trinity at work. The three parts that make up man's spirit are our conscience, our intuition, and communication with God. These three together give us a God consciousness. Notice in 1 Thes 5:23 the order in which the trinity of man is exposed. "May God himself, the God of peace, sanctify you through and through. May your whole spirit, soul and body be kept blameless at the coming of our Lord Jesus Christ" (1 Thes. 5:23 NIV). The temple of man should operate in the order that it is listed in this scripture. The spirit of man after and while communicating with the Holy Spirit of God gains instruction by way of the minister of the sanctuary. This enables the soul (mind) of man to inform the body of the instructions given by the spirit. Again all this happens in a split second. We pray and the Holy Spirit convict's our spirit that a brother is hurting. The Holy Spirit by way of our spirit calls our mind (soul) to remembrance of the word of God, "we must bear our burden one to another." Then our mind tells our body to get up and go help our brother. Most of the time, however, we don't work in the order that we see in 1 Thes. 5:23. Because we refuse to die to self quite often we find the spirit of man is dead in trespasses and isn't communicating with the Holy Spirit. Due to this condition we find the soul of man controls him and throws him into a life of ideas and vain imaginations, or the lust and habits of the flesh provoke him and reduce his soul to slavery. So in most cases we find the order backward, body, soul, and spirit.

The first part we want to examine is the conscience. It is like the compass of an airplane it helps keep us on the narrow path to Heaven. Our conscience is a very strong part of the spirit, for it does not sway to outside influences. If we go against the moral right, the conscience will scream out its voice of insinuation. The conscience is one of conviction. Let me list all the scriptures that pertain to the conscience of man's spirit Ps. 34:18; 51:10; Duet. 2:30; Jn. 13:21; Acts 17:16; Rom. 8:16; 2 Cor. 2:13.

We find that intuition is the hardest of the three to explain because it is the sensing and perceiving part of the spirit. What makes this so difficult is the fact that we sometimes mistake our physical senses or our intellectual senses for the senses of the spirit. It is the exact opposite of these senses. The senses of intuition are direct. They are void of outside influence. That information that comes to us without any direct imputes from the brain or emotions and feelings is said to come to us intuitively. To put this more simply, we gain the knowledge through intuition; our brain merely helps to clarify our understanding of the knowledge we received. What knowledge are we taking about? The revelation of God's word and the knowledge of the work of the Holy Spirit; that is the knowledge. All revelation and work of the Holy Spirit comes through intuition.

In Mark 2:8, we see Jesus utilizing His intuition, "Immediately Jesus knew in his spirit that this was what they were thinking in their hearts, and he said to them, 'Why are you thinking these things?'" (NIV). Jesus gained instant knowledge about what they were thinking. His brain clarified that knowledge. Then His body by way of His mouth spoke saying, "Why are you thinking these things?" Let me list some of the other scriptures that pertain to the intuition of man Matt. 26:41; Mark 2:8; 8:12; John 11:33; Acts 18:25; 20:22; 2 Cor. 7:13.

The last part of the trinity of man's spirit we will discuss is that of communication. Communication with God comes by way of worship. Our soul, what we know as our mind, is incapable of worshipping God. Our intellect cannot reach the heights of Heaven, and therefore cannot express those things. Our flesh cannot feel the depths of God's mercy, and therefore cannot express those feelings. Worship of an awesome, living God only comes through our spirit. This is what John 4:23 confirms for us, "But the hour cometh, and now is, when the true worshippers shall worship the Father in spirit and in truth: for the Father seeketh such to worship him" (KJV). Did you see that last part, the Father seeks this kind of worshipper. He doesn't want us to worship him in our feelings and emotions! NO! He wants us to worship Him in spirit.

BRING IT ALL TOGETHER

All of that having been said how does this work in a practical sense, and what does it look like in action. All of this knowledge in itself means nothing. Remember our formula for wisdom. We must put application with the knowledge gained to produce the result of wisdom.

The first thing we do is re-boot our computer called the brain. All you computer savvy individuals know that if the computer has bad files in it, you reboot the system. That takes out the old files and replaces it with good, new files. That is the first thing we must do in our lives. This is accomplished be putting the word of God into our memory files. That is where "study to show yourself approved" comes in. Next we ignore our feelings and emotions enabling us to not take things personally. This is where dying to yourself comes into play. Then we listen for the spirit to bring to remembrance the word of God that applies to the situation. This is where intuition of our spirit and communion with the Holy Spirit comes into play. Then we act upon the knowledge that was intuitively given through the spirit and clarified by our soul. As you will see in the next few chapters, each step above relates to a specific piece of the armor given to us by God.

6

The Armor

"Put on the whole armour of God, that ye may be able to stand against the wiles of the devil." Eph 6:11 (KJV)

In order to fully understand what Paul is saying, we must render the proper translation to the word armor. The word armor comes from the word *panoplia*, which when translated, means not only the armor you wear for protection from the enemy, but also includes the weapons you use to fight the enemy. It might be better expressed today as the arsenal that God has given us to defeat the enemy of our souls. You might take notice of the fact that Paul when listing the armor included weapons such as the sword and the lance. It scripture should read, to take on the full arsenal of God, that we can stand against the wiles of the Devil.

Armor is of little use without first being put on, and weapons are of little use outside of trained hands. When I was in the military, we had what was called a state of readiness. That was where you had all of your gear packed and ready to ship out on a moment's notice. The problem came when you hadn't been called to deploy for a long time. You would forget where you put some, if not most, of you gear. Then if you got called in the middle of the night you would find yourself in a mad panic, scrambling around to find everything. So it is in the Christian faith. We are told here in this verse to put on the full armor. Notice it didn't say, have ready to put on. The words are very clear, "PUT ON THE FULL ARMOR!"

King Jesus is not asking anything unreasonable of us. The commander of the Kingdom of Heaven itself has followed His own command in wearing of the armor. Hear the words of Isaiah. "And he saw that there was no man, and wondered that there was no intercessor: therefore his arm brought salvation unto him; and his righteousness, it sustained him. For he put on righteousness as a breastplate, and an helmet of salvation upon his head; and he put on the garments of vengeance for clothing, and was clad with zeal as a cloak" (Isa. 59:16-17 KJV).

God looked down and saw no man to intercede on man's behalf. So He sent His son Jesus, who brought salvation to man. Not only salvation that was man-ward, but also righteousness that was God-ward! As if that weren't enough, He went farther by sustaining both. How did King Jesus do this? He did this by doing exactly what He is telling us to do in Eph. 6:11, that is by putting on the full armor.

Reading the passage from Isaiah again, we find the how of this story, "For he put on righteousness as a breastplate, and an helmet of salvation upon his head; and he put on the garments of vengeance for clothing, and was clad with zeal as a cloak."

You are probably thinking, "Jesus needed salvation?" Yes! As we already alluded to the cup that Jesus wanted to pass from Him in the garden of Gethsemane was not the cross per say, but the separation that was coming. Jesus needed the helmet of salvation to sustain Him through that period of separation from the rest of the Trinity.

This passage of scripture in Ephesians 6:11 is not one of a request. The word of God is not saying, "hey you, do you mind putting this on?" The king isn't saying, "you might want to think about wearing this." Make no mistake, the Commander and King of Heaven is issuing a standing order, put on the full armor! This command does not leave it up to every Christian's inclination as to what weapons he or she will put on. That would only bring confusion. We as Christian soldiers are bound by the command to put on the full armor.

Just two verses later, Paul restated the King's position on this issue of the armor, "Wherefore take unto you the whole armor of God, that ye may be able to withstand in the evil day, and having done all, to stand" Eph. 6:13 (KJV). What Paul is saying is, "if you do not obey the command you will not stand against the Devil's schemes and plans." Paul is telling us that the army of the Lord has no place for conscientious objectors. Nor does it have room for soldiers who are AWOL.

Enlisting for the benefits of Heaven is great. Keep in mind brothers and sisters that we have enlisted in a Kingdom at war. We are in a Kingdom with a kingdom arrayed against us.

We could make a separate book of each piece of the armor, but that is not the intent of this labor. We shall but plant seeds firmly in the ground of the hearts and minds of the reader.

If you are dressed and fitted with the armor we will proceed to the weapons training grounds. We will start our first lesson, that of the Loin Belt of Truth.

7

The Loin Belt of Truth

"having your loins girt about with truth."
Eph. 6:14 (KJV)

How applicable that Paul should start with the loin belt of truth. In fact, we see Paul mention the entire armor in order of possession. Notice you can't have righteousness without first having truth. Indeed, what kind of righteousness you will have depends on the kind of truth you possess. Luke 18:9 says that certain individuals had truth in themselves and thought they were righteous. "And he spake this parable unto certain which trusted in themselves that they were righteous, and despised others" (KJV). Then in Matt. 5:20, we are told to "exceed the righteousness of the scribes and Pharisees" (KJV). How do we accomplish this? By girding ourselves with the right kind of truth. Therefore Paul lists the loin belt of truth first.

The loin belt of truth is where we get our strategy. Any good military mind can attest that without truth there can be no good strategy. No Army commander can make battle plans without intelligence information being timely and truthful. False information would cost time, resources, and lives. The same can be said of Christianity. As we rely on the Holy Spirit to quicken our minds to the truth of the word of God. This enables us to know what course of action to take in any given situation. If we are given false information by way of self, Satan, or the world it could cost us time, resources, and perhaps our very souls.

Our loin belt of truth comes from the word of God. I cannot stress this fact enough. You must know the word of God. We no longer can spiritually survive on the regurgitated bread from the pulpits of America. You must study yourselves, whereby you can be found approved by the Holy Spirit. We must know the fundamental truths of the word of God, those truths are the very foundation of our faith in Christ. We should not build our house of faith on sand. It should be built on the solid foundation of the word of God. We should know the practical truths of God, those truths that are like bread and water to our daily lives.

Look at Acts 17:11. "These were more noble than those in Thessalonica, in that they received the word with all readiness of mind, and searched the scriptures daily, whether those things were so" (KJV). Look at what made these people noble. They listened and accepted what was being preached to them. Notice they didn't just stop at the regurgitated word from Paul. They immediately when home and searched the scriptures for themselves, to see if it were true. In essence, they studied to show themselves approved, and through this study at the prompting of Paul they believed. If we study for ourselves, we build a foundation stone that is far less likely to erode with storms of adversity. However, the hearsay from the pulpit can easily be snatched from us.

The second thing I want to point out is that we are not only to know the word, but gird ourselves with it. The word gird means to bind around or prepare for something. In the context of the passage here in Ephesians it means to prepare oneself for war utilizing the truth of God's word. We are to have the word of God, in the files of our mind in such a way that it is like steel girders of a high-rise building. Only by having truth in such a way can righteousness be obtained.

The last thing I wish us to consider about this passage is where it says we are to be girded. It states we are to be girded about the loins. This armor was for the lower parts of the body. If you have ever talked to a football player or perhaps played the game yourself, you know protection of the lower body parts is extremely important. A blow to the loins can be worse than

death itself. When you played football and forgot the protection of your loins, it didn't take long to remember. The first
time you tackled someone you knew you wanted protection.
Look at Isa. 45:1 and see this truth, "and I will loose the loins
of kings, to open before him the two leaved gates; and the gates
shall not be shut" (KJV). Again in Job we see God "weaken the
strength of the mighty" (Job 12:21 KJV).

Let us therefore study that we may be girded about! Let us
not be found weak but strong in the Lord.

8

Breastplate of Righteousness

"and having on the breastplate of righteousness;"
(Eph. 6:14) (KJV)

Here we find the second piece of armor afforded the Christian soldier. The material of this breastplate is that of righteousness. The first question we must ask is what is righteousness? The second is why a breastplate?

Let's look for a moment at the second question of why the breastplate? The breastplate Paul was looking at when he wrote about the armor was that of a Roman soldier. The breastplate he wore covered both front and back. It was made of overlapping strips of metal. When the soldier walked the strips would rub together causing them to become shiny. That shininess of the soldier's breastplate became an offensive weapon as well as defended the parts of the body. If you were going into battle you would want to avoid the guy with the shiny breastplate because he was an experienced veteran soldier. You would want to find the soldier with the dull breastplate in hopes of a better chance of victory. What a gloriously beautiful picture Paul paints for us. As we become identified with Christ through our relationship with Him, the Holy Spirit bears fruit of a Christ-like character. That Christ-like characters shines out from us like that breastplate of steel. Our breastplate of righteousness becomes an offensive weapon against the enemy. As the Son of a living God shines off of our right standing in Christ, then we become light into a darkened world.

[handwritten margin note: Roman soldiers had no back protection. No defense if running]

That brings us back to the first question of what is righteousness? Righteousness is an upright living that is holy according to God's authoritative standard. In Gen. 18:25, we find that God is the one that sets the standard. "That be far from thee to do after this manner, to slay the righteous with the wicked: and that the righteous should be as the wicked, that be far from thee: Shall not the Judge of all the earth do right?"(KJV). From this we see that God says what is righteousness and what is wickedness. We find in Deut 32:4 that it is God that is just and right and we must set our standard to His, and not the other way around. Our definition of righteousness must match God's.

For our definition let's look at Rom. 3:21-22. "But now the righteousness of God without the law is manifested, being witnessed by the law and the prophets; Even the righteousness of God which is by faith of Jesus Christ unto all and upon all them that believe: for there is no difference" (KJV). In plain English, righteousness is a right standing in God, through a right relationship with Christ, and not a right standing with the law! Remember that the law was but a shadow! Even in this shadow there could be found righteousness or better said a right standing through obedience to the law. The Bible even talks about the Pharisees having a righteousness, but their righteousness is with religion and not with a Holy God. We should strive for righteousness in Christ! We should hunger after a Christ-like character, which is the work the Holy Spirit started at our new birth.

This thing of righteousness is of the utmost importance to the success of our warfare. With that said, we have a need to look deeply into this subject for fear of falling short of the objectives set before us in faith. When I talk of righteousness here I am not speaking of that righteousness that is imputed at the regeneration of the new birth. This is done by grace, for see what Paul tells us in Rom. 4:6, "Even as David also described the blessedness of the man, unto whom God imputeth righteousness without works," (KJV). It is this imputed righteousness that restores the love of God to man that was lost at Adam's fall. This imputed righteousness is given by grace and that in the very life of Christ.

The righteousness that we shall uncover here is the re-imparted righteousness that restores the lost image of God to man.

This image was also lost at the fall of Adam, but restored by the work of the Holy Spirit by way of the death and resurrection of Jesus Christ. If man can impart his nature and likeness into a child, how much more can God impart His nature and likeness through the divine workings of the Holy Spirit? It is this divine working of the Holy Spirit that creates for us this breastplate of righteousness.

Righteousness is equated to our stand in Christ. Our stand in a Christ-like character is what will get us persecuted. Matt. 5:10 shares this thought with us, "blessed are they which are persecuted for righteousness' sake: for theirs is the kingdom of heaven" (KJV). Notice it didn't say for religion's sake. Many a Christian has fallen to this deception of the enemy. It didn't say blessed are you because your Baptist, Methodist, etc. denominational beliefs are being persecuted. Look carefully at what Jesus said in Matt. 5:20. "For I say unto you, that except your righteousness shall exceed the righteousness of the scribes and Pharisees, ye shall in no case enter into the kingdom of heaven" (KJV). You see the Scribes and the Pharisees had righteousness, but it was a righteousness based on a right standing with the church, and not with Jesus Christ. I fear to many of us have good or right standing in the church, but fail to have a right standing in Christ.

I am convinced that this divine working of the Holy Spirit in the life of every Christian is initiated and intensified by the pursuit of an intimate relationship with the person of Jesus Christ. Jesus does not want us to be a lifeless instrument like a guitar in the hand of a musician. He wants us to be a living child in the hand of the father through the power of the Holy Spirit. Matt. 5:6 tells us "blessed are those who hunger and thirst for righteousness, for they will be filled." He is not speaking of that imputed righteousness that is deposited in our account at the new birth. He is referring to another righteousness or else it wouldn't have stated we should hunger and thirst after it. He is alluding to a righteousness that is in Christ or brought about through a relationship with Christ. The term "in Christ" is mentioned 99 times in the New Testament. The only way to be in Christ is to pursue a relationship with Christ by the power of the Holy Spirit.

I want to divert our attention and spend a little time discussing the pursuit of a relationship with Christ. I feel this is the second of the three keys to success in our spiritual warfare. We already found the first key is knowing the word of God. The second is having a relationship with Jesus Christ. Not just any relationship, but an intimate relationship. I am not talking about an acquaintance, someone you know about. We can say easily that we know about Jesus. We know where he was born and the miracles He performed. However knowing about someone and knowing someone are two totally separate things are they not? To know someone you must be able to tell what he or she is going to do under given circumstances. For example, when I was dating my wife of now seven years, I could tell you her favorite color and food. Now I can tell you how she is going to react if I forget to lift the toilet seat, or go out and spend hundreds of dollars without telling her about it. You see I know how she is going to react in sickness or in despair. That is called really knowing somebody. How did I reach that level of knowledge about my wife? Simple, I spent time with her in all kinds of situations.

I don't want you to get the idea that we are constantly chasing Jesus down saying, "excuse me, oh, excuse me." Like we have to gain his attention or affection. That would be the furthest thing from the truth. Jesus is chasing you through the conviction of the Holy Spirit saying, "HELLO! OH HELLO! can you stop long enough to talk with me." I know what you're thinking, I have so much crud and stuff in my life Jesus is probably running away from me! If you smell smoke right about now, that's because that statement reeks of smoke. It comes straight from the kingdom of darkness. Listen to 1 Jn. 4:19, "we love him, because he first loved us" (KJV).

To better understand God's desire for intimacy look at Genesis chapter 2–3. Here we find God walking in the garden with Adam. God even paraded all living creatures in front of Adam just for the sole purpose of seeing what Adam would name them. I can imagine God looking at Adam and laughing when Adam named the baboon. He probable said where did you come up with that name. It's the same as with my three-year-old son, Eric, and myself. I came home and Eric was upset with his four-year-old brother, Jared. Eric said, "I wish you would quit being so melodramatic." It was very difficult not to roll over laughing, because where did a three-year-old learn of melodramatic, and did he even know what that meant. Come to find out he did and that was even more hilarious. I can picture Adam and God's relationship like that. God rolling over with laughter and saying, where did you come up with baboon. Some of the names Adam gave were understandable like woman. That was the first thought I had when I saw for the first time the beauty of my wife. I said to myself, "woooman, God is good!" So I can see where others would have been quite comical. The point being that they had an intimate relationship.

Look at chapter 3, here we see that man and woman have sinned. You would think God would be very angry with them. I mean, God gave them the utmost liberty in the garden with respect to what they could do and eat. He only said this one thing don't do. Then the very thing God had told them not to do they did. The one thing and only one thing they were not to do they did. How many of us get mad at our children for the same thing? However in verse 8 of chapter 3 we see God doing the complete opposite. He walks through the garden in the cool of the evening just like He had done everyday before this one. The only difference is that man is hiding. It is not like God couldn't have gone right to man's hiding place and said, "DIDN'T I TELL YOU NOT TO DO THAT?" He could have yelled and screamed, but instead he called out to Adam in the same soft voice as every other day. It was God who went looking for Adam. God still wanted intimacy with Adam, but Adam ran the other way and hid. Jesus even today calls unto us with the same voice saying, "Where are you? Come back." Jesus knows where we are, but is giving us the opportunity to come freely unto Him. As we study the word of God, we begin to understand how God reacts under given circumstances. That gives us intimacy. Now you can see why the breastplate of righteousness is tied to the loin belt of truth. Without the truth of the word of God we can never hope to gain intimacy with Jesus Christ. Without intimacy with Jesus Christ we can never hope to achieve righteousness.

9

Shoes of Preparation of the Gospel

"And your feet shod with the preparation of the gospel of peace;" Eph. 6:15 (KJV)

Let's start our discussion with the shoes Paul was viewing while writing this. They were leather sandal-type shoes that had shin guards made into them. They also had steel spikes on the soles of the shoes. They not only protected the soldier's feet but also gave a sure footing when walking on rough terrain. They could also be used as an offensive weapon by kicking or stepping on the enemy.

Why does Paul relate the preparation of the gospel to that of shoes? The word preparation comes from the word *hetoimasia*, which translated means a person in a condition so advanced that they are in a state of preparedness or readiness. In the military we conducted what they call readiness training. This training was to prepare all soldiers for any type of battle situation. One thing I learned from those exercises was that there came a great amount of confidence and peace with being prepared. Think back for a moment to when you where in school. Remember when it was test time, the fear and trepidation that came with not being pre-pared. Oh, but when you were prepared how different you felt. What peace and confidence abounded in you?

Notice that this verse doesn't say having our feet shod with the *spreading* of the gospel in peace. No, it says having our feet shod with the "*preparation* of the gospel." Sometimes I think we run out of camp without our shoes. Quite often we are so eager to run out and spread the gospel of the Kingdom that we forget to prepare the gospel in our own hearts. The amount of time required for victory and/or defeat is directly proportional to the amount of time spent in preparation. Short in preparation, quick to defeat! Long in preparation, quick to victory! Preparation comes from study, and study the word of God we must. Study gives us knowledge, while training gives us application of the knowledge, whereby wisdom is gained.

Hear what Timothy tells us of preparation, "study to shew thyself approved unto God, a workman that needeth not to be ashamed, rightly dividing the word of truth" (2 Tim. 2:15 KJV). The word approved here in Timothy refers to silver or precious metal being tried in the refiner's fire to be true. Readiness training in the military meant that you conducted exercises in all that you had learned, whereby you could refine that knowledge into perfection. So it is with us spiritually. As we walk through our daily lives, they become exercises in the knowledge of the word of God. Those exercises bring us to a state of readiness or a preparation of the good news of the Kingdom of Heaven. That readiness and preparation allows you to always be able to "give an answer to every man that ask you a reason of the hope that is in you" (1 Pet. 3:15).

Now we can see why Paul calls this the gospel of peace. It is the thorough knowledge of the word of God working everyday in our lives that brings true lasting peace to our lives. Only when we apply the laws and principles of a living God to our lives can we fully feel the blessing from a living God flow out from our lives. Oh, what glorious peace there is to know that when you are free in Jesus, you are free indeed!

Next let's focus on what gospel Paul is referencing here in Ephesians. We get a glimpse of what Paul is telling us by the fact he says it is a gospel of peace. True peace comes only through the reconciling work of Jesus Christ. Colossians 1:22 says, "But now he has reconciled you by Christ's physical body through death to present you holy in his sight, without blemish and free from accusation" (NIV). Being free from accusation brings peace. How is this accomplished? This is done through the reconciling ministry of Jesus Christ.

We find in 2 Cor. 5:18, "all this is from God, who reconciled us to himself through Christ and gave us the ministry of reconciliation." What is this ministry of reconciliation? It is to share "that God was reconciling the world to himself in Christ, not counting men's sins against them." It goes on to state; "and he has committed to us the message of reconciliation." The word message there is the same word *gospel.* We find ourselves prepared through being reconciled daily through the study of God's word. Verse 20 reels this in for us by stating, "we are therefore Christ's ambassadors, as though God we're making his appeal through us. We implore you on Christ's behalf: Be reconciled to God."

Jesus' whole ministry was that of peace through reconciliation of man to God. That is why in the gospels of Matthew and John we see Jesus riding into town on a donkey (Matt. 21:5; John 12:14). When a king conquered a city through peace, the king would ride into town on a donkey. That is why John 12:15 says "do not be afraid, O Daughter of Zion; see, your king is coming, seated on a donkey's colt," Do not be afraid because the king is coming in peace. If you saw the king riding into town on a white horse then you would be afraid, for the white horse symbolized a conquering king, a king who had won the city through war. This is how we shall see Christ return in the book of Revelation. We can meet Christ at the peace table of reconciliation, or we can meet him on the battlefield of sin. Let us all securely fasten the shoes of preparation, that we may walk in the newness of the Kingdom at hand, fully prepared for the ministry of reconciliation.

10

Shield of Faith

Above all, taking the shield of faith, wherewith ye shall be able to quench all the fiery darts of the wicked. Eph. 6:16 (KJV)

The scripture here tells us to take the shield of faith. It does not tell us to go out and find or acquire a shield of faith. The word used here implies that a shield is being offered and you merely take it. "Looking unto Jesus the author and finisher of our faith," we know from this scripture that Jesus is the one who freely offers us the shield of faith. Laying hold to the gift of faith is an absolute necessity to the subject of spiritual warfare. In fact it is impossible to please God in our Christian walk without having the shield of faith (Heb. 11:6).

Not everyone takes this free gift. We find others that do not appropriate and maintain that shield. Look at this truth stated in God's word, "And pray that we may be delivered from wicked and evil men, for not everyone has faith" (2 Thess. 3:2 NIV). Did you catch that? It says "that we may be delivered." He's talking about Christians, not the unsaved or else he would have said they instead of we. He is saying here that not all Christians have faith. Are we then saying that Jesus didn't give the gift of faith to some Christians? NO! What it is saying is that not all Christians took the gift of faith. Without the shield of faith we would not be able to follow our intuition because intuition requires belief in the unseen. We must have the shield of faith in order to utilize intuition.

I remember one time when my wife and I were going to buy a car. Everything logically speaking seemed to add up. The payment was right (very low), the interest rate seemed good (if that's possible), and it was just the right size and color for our growing family. Then my wife speaks the dreaded words something about this doesn't feel or seem right. You know, it was a good deal everything physically speaking was right. So at that moment I was thinking to myself, this would be a good time for her to die to herself, you know those feelings and emotions. I know, I should be ashamed of myself, and I was because through the prompting of the Holy Spirit conviction came by way of my conscience. I realized these were not external feelings driven by her senses. These feelings came from deep within her spirit. Her intuition was telling her this isn't good for the future. You see, only God knows the future, and only God knew how this purchase was going to affect our future. My wonderful wife had to have faith in something that she couldn't tangibly put her hands on. To my good fortune I listened to her intuition and we didn't buy the vehicle. Later that year I was out of work for six months and that car payment would have devastated us. Praise God for intuition and a godly wife that listens! As you read on take hold of the gift of faith.

The shield Paul was looking at when he wrote this passage was unique. This shield was about four feet tall, and was made of fifteen layers of leather. The leather was held together by a band of iron around the edge. It then had an iron handle on the back. Sometimes it had the family crest on the front. In order for the shield to be maintained the soldier had to apply a small amount of oil to the front of the leather everyday. This kept the leather from becoming hard and brittle. The oil would also help extinguish any flame that hit it. This process of applying the oil was painstaking, and time-consuming. You had to apply just the right amount at the right times. What a beautiful illustration Paul gives us of faith. Even though the shield was freely given to the soldier he still had to work to keep it. Even though faith is freely given to the Christian we must apply the oil of works to our faith every day of our lives. Let's examine together how we accomplish this task.

The productive Christian life is always proportional to the scope and power of real faith. A Christian must have faith in God's work of the past, present, and future, and desire to make it a vital part of his or her life experience. The Holy Spirit is at work trying to produce in us the nature and character of Christ, and His tool is not logic but faith. We often hear people say, you've just got to have faith, but those same people can't tell you how to get faith or make it functional and practical in your life. My prayer is that the Holy Spirit will reveal to us a faith that "pleases God."

The first thing we must know about faith is that, like every-thing else that is vital to the Christian walk, it is not something we work to obtain but is a free gift (Eph. 2:8). Faith is like all the other gifts of God. He tells us how to get them and how to properly use them in order to have success. Faith in every case wherever it exists, without exception is the gift of God (Gal. 5:22). Since we know this fact to be true the question that raises itself to us is this: How do we appropriate the gift of faith?

In order to appropriate faith we must acquire a working knowl-edge of God's word, because as we are told, faith comes by the word. "So then faith cometh by hearing, and hearing by the word of God" (Rom. 10:17 KJV). Faith, as we know it, is a law. What makes it a law is that it is universal. It works in every city, state, and country. The word faith means belief without proof. So you can have faith even without using the word of God. Let me give you an example.

If you tell a child they are stupid long enough that child will begin to have faith in your words. There was a study done on first graders. One day they told them that all blue-eyed kids were smarter and better than the brown-eyed kids. This went on all day thruough all their activities. The blue-eyed kids got to go to lunch first etc. At the end of the day, they gave them a test. The blue-eyed kids scored higher on the test. The next day they told the children they had made a mistake and that all brown-eyed kids were smarter and better than the blue-eyed kids. They went through the same exercises and then gave them the same test from the day before. This time the brown-eyed kids scored higher. Those kids believed in words with no proof. In essence they had faith in what was told to them.

The principle of faith is a law. This is why I must be mind-ful of what I hear. Remember that what we hear gets put into the files of our soul. So if you want the right kind of faith be mindful of what you hear. I would also point out that reading the word isn't equivalent to hearing the word. It is always a good idea to read the Bible out loud as often as possible. Faith is an utter dependence and belief in the faithfulness of God and an absolute dependence upon His word and promises. Faith finds no comfort or assurance in anything except the word of God. The more you know the word the more hope you will have to be able to grow from a "measure of faith" to a "great faith." Faith takes the words and promises of God and claims them as its own. The more of the word it hears the more seeds it has for a potentially great harvest. Faith can have everything stolen from it, but these three words, "it is written." To believers who have studied to show themselves approved, never can those three words be stripped from their lips!

Just the possessions of seeds does not produce a crop. This truth is stated in Hebrews 4:2, "For unto us was the gospel preached, as well as unto them: but the word preached did not profit them, not being mixed with faith in them that heard it" (KJV). We can see from this scripture that we need something else to be added to our hearing. That leads us to the second part of appropriating the gift of faith.

The second step to faith is to believe the word that we have heard. This is called the sprouting of the seed of faith. Believing is far more than just hearing and acknowledging what you have heard. Believing is having such a trust, assurance, and reliance upon what you heard that you are led to commit your life to it. We read in Galatians 3:11 that "the just shall live by faith." By this we see that faith is more than just mental; it must have life and this life comes when we start believing what we know. Believing dissolves the outer shell of the seed and lets the inner life spring forth.

Paul states it this way, the word will only be effective in you when you believe (1 Thess. 2:13). Paul also told us that hearing the word and not mixing belief with it is ineffective and unprofitable (Heb. 4:2). Far too often we know more than we believe, and the good seeds go to waste. I hope you can see that you must add belief to knowledge. Jesus gives us a great example of the connection between belief and knowledge in the healing of the blind man when he said, "believe that I am able to do this" (Matt. 9:28). The blind man must have had knowledge of Jesus ability to heal. Note Jesus didn't ask where or how had he heard of His ability to heal. Jesus just asked, "Do you believe?" The man needed to add belief to his knowledge.

Now we have come to the third step to faith, that of confessing what we know and believe. This is called the growth of faith. If we desire our faith to grow, then we must confess with our mouth what we know in our head and believe with our heart. This step of faith is pictured in Romans 10:8; "But what saith it? The word is nigh thee, even in thy mouth, and in thy heart: that is, the word of faith" (KJV). Confession is to acknowledge with our mouth what we know to be true through our life. Paul calls it "holding forth the word of life" (Phil. 2:16). Confessing with our mouth should be an outward testimony of an inward reality. This will also increase our hearing, which results in growth. Paul states this step of faith very clearly. "It is written: I believed; therefore I have spoken." With that same spirit of faith we also believe and therefore speak," (2 Cor. 4:13 NIV). The Bible most definitely teaches that confession is essential to faith. Look at these scriptures that confirm this. "Whosoever therefore shall confess me before men, him will I confess also before my Father which is in heaven" (Matt. 10:32 KJV). "For with the heart man believeth unto righteousness; and with the mouth confession is made unto salvation" (Rom. 10:10 KJV). These are just a few of the verses that show the necessity of confession. If we desire a strong, growing, and victorious faith then we must confess the word of God in every situation where faith is needed. If you truly want victory over Satan's kingdom, you must know the word, believe the word, and confess the word.

We have now come to the fourth and final step of faith. The fourth step is one of acting on what you know, believe, and have confessed. This is called the fruit of faith. We find this step of faith in the book of James, "So speak ye, and so do"(KJV). James also says "be ye doers of the word, and not hearers only, deceiving your own selves" (James 1:22 KJV). In other words, you shall have fruit if you are not someone who just says the word, but is also a doer of the word. If you know the word to be true, then confess the word as truth. Then you must act upon it in daily living. Faith is not only a gift it is a duty to be acted on. Belief is not enough, the "Devil believes also and trembles." As Christians we should desire to please our Heavenly Father. This is accomplished by translating our belief and words into actions. It is when faith is moved from your head to your heart and released through your hands in daily living that results are obtained. We are told that; "faith without works is dead," meaning fruitless (James 14).

Faith cannot be passive, it must be active or it is not faith. All through the Bible we see examples of how God's children, by putting faith into action, are able to accomplish great and mighty deeds. Great things were accomplished by ordinary men and women who knew the word, believed the word, and then acted upon the word. The result of this kind of faith is "the substance of things hoped for, the evidence of things not seen." This is indeed the faith that pleases God, and should be the desire of our heart.

Faith is the compendium of all Christian virtues. It is the index of all that pertains to the Christian life. It is the channel through which all that God has passes through to us. All our labors, self-denial, fasting and church-goings count for nothing without faith. We must, therefore, always be making advances in our faith. We should go from faith in its beginnings to faith in its perfection, where we learn to introduce it into everything we do. We should come to a place where faith becomes the atmosphere in which we live, the air in which our spirit breathes. Faith should not be our dessert, but the very bread of life. Faith should not be our holy clothing for special occasions, but our everyday dress. Faith should bring us to the point where we trust not in things within, or things without, but in the things above.

You can have this kind of faith. It is a gift; the shield is given freely to you. However once you have the shield you must apply the oil upon it daily by knowing, believing, confessing, and acting on the word of God. Without this we cannot please God. So take what He has given and learn of it and then use it to His honor and glory and your reward.

11

Helmet of Salvation

"And take the helmet of salvation," Eph. 6:17 (KJV)

So far we have discovered that the loin belt of truth is where we get our strategy and the breastplate of righteousness is our standard. Also we saw that having our feet shod with preparation was our walk, and the shield of faith is our protection. Now we shall reveal our hope that is in the helmet of our salvation.

The first thing we must uncover about this passage is what salvation Paul is talking about here in Ephesians. Looking at the helmet Paul was viewing while writing this passage might shed some light on this topic for us. The helmet was the prettiest of the entire armor, especially the centurion soldier's helmet. Of all the graces that can be bestowed upon His children, salvation is the prettiest of them all. The helmet protected the soldier's head. How much also should we protect our souls from the sword of the enemy powers? The helmet also protected the ears. Should we not also protect what we hear that we may have a proper faith in Christ?

Let me embark on this topic; by first stating why I feel this passage is not talking about our eternal salvation, but our daily salvation. I believe that eternal salvation is the most beautiful thing given us, however it's put on once and secured in us through the blood of Jesus Christ. The helmet that is referred to in this passage is put on daily. We should not be questioning our eternal security daily, for we are told that it is secure in Christ. "How shall we escape if we ignore such a great salvation? This salvation, which was first announced by the Lord, was confirmed to us by those who heard him" (Heb. 2:3 NIV). We cannot as the scripture says ignore this great gift of eternal salvation.

We can also know through scripture that our eternal salvation is secure. "Therefore I endure all things for the elect's sakes, that they may also obtain the salvation which is in Christ Jesus with eternal glory" (2 Tim. 2:10 KJV). Here is what 2 Cor. 6:1–2 tells us, "For he saith, I have heard thee in a time accepted, and in the day of salvation have I secured thee: behold, now is the accepted time; behold, now is the day of salvation" (KJV). What Paul is saying here is that the day you accepted the blood of Jesus Christ He secured you with eternal salvation. He goes on in verses 4 through 10 to express all the daily afflictions we, through the same grace and workings of the Holy Spirit, shall be saved from and through. That salvation will come daily. Here in Ephesians, Paul is stressing that we put on the helmet of salvation to meet our daily trials and tribulations, rather than to obtain our eternal security. A soldier that was issued a helmet did not put it on once and leave it securely fastened forever. The soldier had to daily put on the helmet or else lose his protection for that day. This is why we read in Phil. 2:12, "continue to work out your salvation with fear and trembling." Let me give you an example in hopes of shedding some light on this subject. A fighter pilot is given a free gift of training and knowledge of how to fly a jet fighter. In addition he is given a thirty million-dollar aircraft to fly. We, like that pilot, are given the training and knowledge of how to operate effectively in the Kingdom of Heaven. We are then given a new temple bought with the priceless blood of Jesus Christ to operate in. Even though the pilot has been freely given the training, knowledge, and aircraft he still must work out all of that, to survive the dangers of combat that day. We are no different than the pilot. Just because we have the new temple, training and knowledge, we must also work all of that out in order to sustain us through the daily perils of life. We must put on the helmet of salvation daily.

Let Paul fortify this position for us. He tells us in 1 Thess. 5:8, "putting on the breastplate of faith and love; and for an helmet, the hope of salvation" (KJV). Listen, I no longer hope for eternal security for it is a reality! Brothers and sisters in Christ if you do not believe your eternal salvation is secure read carefully the following scriptures:

> Surely it is you who love the people; all the holy ones are in your hand. At your feet they all bow down, and from you receive instruction. Deut. 33:3 (NIV)

> And I give unto them eternal life; and they shall never perish, neither shall any man pluck them out of my hand. My Father, which gave them me, is greater than all; and no man is able to pluck them out of my Father's hand. John 10:28–29 (KJV)

Did you see that, it is permanent never to be taken? You, my fellow believers, are firmly in the hand of the father. To hope is to look to the future. How can we look forward to something that is already here and a reality to us? Clearly Paul in 1 Thess. 5:8, says we are to put on the "helmet," that is "the hope of salvation." The only salvation I have yet to obtain and must hope for is the daily salvation from the trials and temptation that self, Satan, and the world are going to throw at me today. What we need daily is a salvation of the soul. Peter concurs with this in 1 Peter 1:9, when he says "even the salvation of your souls."

The grace of salvation provided the believer is like a beautiful diamond, no matter which way you look at the diamond each facet holds the fullness of its rich beauty.

The Bible reveals seven types of salvations (God's complete number), and we need to know and apply the fullness of these salvations to our lives. By viewing all the facets the diamond of grace offers us, can we appreciate the wonders of the helmet!

The first grace of salvation is to be eternally saved before God. We receive this grace the moment we accept Jesus as our Lord and Savior. This salvation affords us the deliverance from judgment of sins, the curse of the law, the punishment of hell, and the power of Satan's Kingdom. It speaks of our being justified, sanctified, and reconciled to God, as well as, our sins being forgiven and our iniquities cleansed. It means we are born again, possessing the eternal life of Christ, with our dead spirits quickened to life and the Holy Spirit indwelling us. This grace of eternal life is accomplished for us by the work of Jesus Christ and not by our works, only by our accepting His completed work.

The next facet is that of sustaining grace of our daily salvation. "Wherefore he is able also to save them to the uttermost that come unto God by him, seeing he ever liveth to make intercession for them" (Heb 7:25 KJV). We know from the above scripture that because Jesus lives forever, he is able to give us daily salvation. This daily salvation is conditional on our drawing near unto Christ.

Following sustaining grace we have delivering grace of salvation from affliction. We have salvation, which provides God's deliverance in special times of afflictions. "Notwithstanding the Lord stood with me, and strengthened me; that by me the preaching might be fully known, and that all the Gentiles might hear: and I was delivered out of the mouth of the lion" (2 Tim. 4:17 KJV). Peter talked a lot about salvation from affliction. Just read 1 Peter and see for yourself. Peter asserts that delivering grace is afforded the believer through identification. As we are identified with Christ through the power of the Holy Spirit, we are also delivered unto God in Heavenly places with Christ. Peter encourages us through the fact that while afflictions are but temporal, our identity is eternal through Christ. We must believe in God's power and provisions to save us out of our afflictions.

Next we have rewarding grace through the salvation of the soul. We already established the fact that we are made in three parts body, soul, and spirit. Our salvation therefore reaches into all three of these areas. The salvation of our soul relates especially to our entering the millennial kingdom and reigning with the Lord, who will reward us and cause our soul to enjoy with Him the joy of the kingdom.

"For whosoever will save his life (soul) shall lose it: and whosoever will lose his life (soul) for my sake shall find it" (Matt. 16:25 KJV). "Save" here does not point to eternal salvation, since the salvation spoken of here is not freely given according to faith. The salvation here requires a cost; losing and sacrificing itself shall save the soul. A saved person who is willing to deny himself, to take up the cross and follow the

Lord, and be willing to sacrifice his own soul shall enter the millennial kingdom (Matt. 25:21-23). All those who lose themselves (die to themselves) that Christ might work through them (ministering to our sanctuary) shall have their souls saved and enjoy the kingdom.

"He that endureth to the end, the same shall be saved" (Matt. 10:22). "But we are not of them who draw back unto perdition; but of them that have faith unto the saving of the soul" (Heb. 10:39 KJV). The "faith" mentioned here is not the faith of entering eternal life, but the faith for our Christian walk. It is not the faith for life, but the faith of faithfulness. If after we are saved, we seek to manifest the work of Christ and His life, our souls shall be saved in the future and we shall have a part of Christ's Kingdom. "Receiving the end of your faith, even the salvation of your souls" (1 Peter 1:9).

"Therefore, get rid of all moral filth and the evil that is so prevalent and humbly accept the word planted in you, which can save you" (James 1:21 NIV). Here again we see that our work is required. Don't panic because of the word works. We have attached such a stigma to the idea of works that we refuse to look at it. The word work that is pertaining to salvation is not a work that is of us. For we know that any work of ourselves is considered dead works (Heb. 6:1). The only work that we perform to be considered living works is that of dying to self. Only by our work of laying self on the brazen altar, can the Holy Spirit produce living works through us. Those living works produced in the believer are the works unto salvation mentioned above. So we can see that this is still grace, for these works are not of self, but imputed by Christ through us in the power of the Holy Spirit.

This work done by the Holy Sprit brings an intimate relationship with Christ. That relationship brings empowering grace through salvation from the world's systems. You will hear more of the world systems in the tactics chapter. We have spoken greatly of this grace at the beginning of this chapter, so we won't cover that again here.

The last grace we will mention is that of promising grace. Promising grace is brought about through family salvation.

"They replied, 'Believe in the Lord Jesus, and you will be saved–you and your household'" (Acts 16:31 NIV). "Crispus, the synagogue ruler, and his entire household believed in the Lord; and many of the Corinthians who heard him believed and were baptized" (Acts 18:8 NIV). "For the promise is unto you, and to your children, and to all that are afar off, even as many as the Lord our God shall call"(Acts 2:39 KJV). We can see from these scriptures that God wants salvation not only for us but promises salvation for our households as well. The grace of God is so great that He wants to extend it to your family.

Oh, the beautiful helmet of salvation. This is the awesome salvation Peter writes about in 1 Peter 1:9–12. It is this fullness of the graces provided us through the love of Jesus Christ that Peter says the prophets inquired of and diligently searched for. It wasn't just eternal salvation that caused the angels to be amazed. It was the blood of Christ, which caused the angels to peer through Heaven with amazement. This precious blood gives us all of the salvations!

Think for a moment of all the graces that have been bestowed upon us. Then think about the price paid for those graces to come. Jesus, who from the beginning of time had been a vital part of a collective called the Trinity of the Father, Son, and Holy Spirit. From the foundations of the universe, Jesus has heard the voice of the cognitive soul of the collective called Father God. Before the foundations of the world, Jesus has felt the life giving force of the collective called the Holy Spirit. There in the garden of Gethsemane, as the weight of the world's sins is bearing down on His shoulders, He begins to feel the separation from the collective. For the first time there is silence from the father. Jesus struggles with the absence of that voice and prays; "Father, if it be possible." Jesus so wanted to go to the cross and save the world. If He could only do that without being separated from the collective of the Trinity. As the umbilical cord is being severed from the Holy Spirit, He again prays. He concedes to the fact this must be and the angel comforts Him giving strength to His faith. Think about the fact that God turn his back on Himself, and you realize the beauty and awe of the helmet of salvation.

A friend of mine sent me an email that best shares the awesome fullness of salvation. Imagine the following:

It's a Wednesday night and you are at a church prayer meeting when somebody runs in from the parking lot and says, "Turn on a radio, turn on a radio." While the church listens to a little transistor radio with a microphone stuck up to it, the announcement is made: "Two women are lying in a Long Island hospital dying from the mystery flu." Within hours it seems, this thing just sweeps across the country. People are working around the clock trying to find an antidote. Nothing is working. California, Oregon, Arizona, Florida, Massachusetts all over the country. It's as though it's just sweeping in from the borders. And then, suddenly the news comes out. The code has been broken. A cure can be found. A vaccine can be made.

It's going to take the blood of somebody who hasn't been infected, and so, sure enough, all through the Midwest, through all those channels of emergency broadcasting, everyone is asked to do one simple thing: "Go to your downtown hospital and have your blood type taken. That's all we ask of you. When you hear the sirens go off in your neighborhood, please make your way quickly, quietly, and safely to the hospitals."

Sure enough, when you and your family get down there late on that Friday night, there is a long line, and they've got nurses and doctors coming out and pricking fingers and taking blood and putting labels on it. Your wife and your kids are out there, and they take your blood type and they say, "Wait here in the parking lot. When we've processed your blood, you can be dismissed and go home." You stand around, scared, with your neighbors, wondering what in the world is going on and if this is the end of the world.

Suddenly a young man comes running out of the hospital screaming. He's yelling a name and waving a clipboard. What? He yells it again! And your son tugs on your jacket and says, "Daddy, that's me."

Before you know it, they have grabbed your boy. Wait a minute. Hold on! And they say, "It's okay, his blood is clean. His blood is pure. We want to make sure he doesn't have the disease. We think he has got the right type."

Five very tense minutes later out come the doctors and nurses, crying and hugging one another—some are even laughing. It's the first time you have seen anybody laugh in a week, and an old doctor walks up to you and says, "Thank you, sir. Your son's blood type is perfect. It's clean, it is pure, and we can make the vaccine." As the word begins to spread all across that parking lot full of folks, people are screaming and praying and laughing and crying.

But then the gray-haired doctor pulls you and your wife aside and says, "May we see you for a moment? We didn't realize that the donor would be a minor and we need... we need you to sign a consent form." You begin to sign and then you see that the number of pints of blood to be taken is empty.

"H-how many pints?"

And that is when the old doctor's smile fades and he says, "We had no idea it would be little child. We weren't prepared. We need it all!"

"But-but..."

"You don't understand. We are talking about the world here.... Please sign. We-we need it all!"

"But can't you give him a transfusion?"

"If we had clean blood we would. Can you sign? Would you sign?" In numb silence, you do.

Then they say, "Would you like to have a moment with him before we begin?" Can you walk back? Can you walk back to that room where he sits on a table saying, "Daddy? Mommy? What's going on?" Can you take his hands and say, "Son, your mommy and I love you, and we would never ever let anything happen to you that didn't just have to be. Do you understand that?"

And when that old doctor comes back in and says, "I'm sorry, we've got to get started. People all over the world are dying." Can you leave? Can you walk out while he is saying, "Dad? Mom? Dad? Why, why have you forsaken me?

And then next week, when they have the ceremony to honor your son, and some folks sleep through it, and some folks don't even come because they went to the lake. Yet other folks come with a pretentious smile and just pretend to care, would you want to jump up and say, "MY SON DIED FOR YOU! DON'T YOU CARE?"

Why does Paul relate this hope of salvation to a helmet? Well we know the helmet protects the head and ears. As we have already discussed the battle is waged in your mind (soul). The helmet relates to protecting the mind. Look at the following scriptures that bring this forward for us. "And have put on the new man, which is renewed in knowledge after the image of him that created him:" (Col. 3:10). "And be renewed in the spirit of your mind;" (Eph. 4:23). "And be not conformed to this world: but be ye transformed by the renewing of your mind, that ye may prove what is that good, and acceptable, and perfect, will of God" (Rom. 12:2).

We need to put on the helmet of salvation to protect the mind from any thought that would "exalt itself against the knowledge of Christ." We need to allow the helmet to fortify the castle of our soul from any vain imaginatings that would capture us from the word of Christ. We need to protect our ears from any vain philosophy and principles of the world that strive to overcome us.

Lastly our eternal security, this thing we call eternal salvation finds its place in the helmet of salvation. Where you ask? It rests solely in the strap that secures the helmet in place. Without the strap how easily does the helmet become disengaged? Rest assured it is your eternal salvation that firmly secures your daily salvation in place. That blessed assurance gives us the fortitude to carry on the battle of daily living. Desire not only eternal salvation, but also press towards the fullness of all the graces afforded you.

12

Sword of the Spirit

"and the sword of the Spirit, which is the word of God:" Ephesians 6:17

Here is the sixth piece of armor brought to the hand of the Christian soldier. So far we have found our strategy in the belt. Our standard came from the breastplate. We found our walk in the shoes. Protection is firmly entrenched in faith. Our hope secured in salvation, and now we discover our weapon of combat. There is a two-fold question we must ask ourselves of this scripture. Why a sword and why relate the word of God to a sword?

The sword is regarded as the most vital part of the soldier's armament. It is extremely embarrassing for a soldier to be found on the battlefield without his weapons. So it is with the word of God. How bad it is on the battlefield of life to be caught without the word of God easily accessible in the mind. The Roman sword was that of a two edged sword. This sword could cut both ways, coming and going. If you didn't know how to properly use such a weapon you could find yourself seriously injured. Matthew 15:11 tells us that it's not necessarily what goes in our mouth that destroys us, but what comes out of our mouth that kills.

The sword, which is the word of God, is a defensive weapon. It is with the word of God that man defends himself from the regiment of temptation. Jesus when tempted of Satan did not say I am God go away. He pulled out the same weapon that you and I have at our disposal. He said, "it is written." Jesus knew that you and I could not say I am God go away. Jesus used the same two-edged sword that you and I have been issued.

Not only is this sword one of defense but also becomes an offensive weapon in that it kills our old nature of sin and lust of the flesh that lurks within us. We read in the gospels of those that escaped the contaminants of the world, yet they were over-taken because the lust of their flesh was not mortified in them by the power of the word applied to their lives. Is this not what we find in 2 Pet. 2:20? "For if after they have escaped the pollu-tions of the world through the knowledge of the Lord and Sav-ior Jesus Christ, they are again entangled therein, and over-come, the latter end is worse with them than the beginning" (KJV). You see they had the sword, that being the knowledge of the word, but did not rightly know how to use the sword.

Next, Jesus, being skilled with the sword, was able too wield it with power. "And they were astonished at his doctrine: for his word was with power" (Luke 4:32 KJV). Not only Jesus, but the apostles also, had power with the sword. Look at Acts chapter 4, where Peter and John had healed a man by the power of the word. In verse 7 we hear the question posed to them "by what power, or by what name, have ye done this?" Again in Acts 4:33, "And with great power gave the apostles witness of the resurrection of the Lord Jesus: and great grace was upon them all."

What gave them such power? I believe we find this answer in the order in which this piece of armor was given. The sword was one of the last things given to a soldier. They had to be skilled in the rest of the armor. The disciplines of the rest of the armor had to be refined and perfected before taking up a sword. Having a sword does not make one a warrior. Some of the children of God are quick to wield the word of God at some-one, while failing to put on the breastplate of righteousness. That person's heart is set on foolish gain and not on the heart of the Lord. "This people draweth nigh unto me with their mouth, and honoureth me with their lips; but their heart is far from me" (Matt. 15:8 KJV).

The sword of the Spirit should never be used in an offen-sive posture against our brothers or sisters in Christ. Yes, I

agree with Timothy in that "all scripture is given by inspiration of God, and is profitable for doctrine, for reproof, for cor-
rection, for instruction in righteousness"(2 Tim. 3:16 KJV).
However be sure that this is done in the manner of righteousness of the love of Christ. We should always "endeavor to keep
the unity of the Spirit in the bond of peace" (Eph. 4:3 KJV). Do
not execute the wounded, remembering always our ministry
of reconciliation.

13

Prayer and Supplication

**"Praying always with all prayer and supplication in
the Spirit, and watching thereunto with all
perseverance and supplication for all saints:
Eph. 6:18 (KJV).**

Prayer is like ammunition to a soldier. To be found on the battlefield of life with no ammunition is dangerous indeed. The Kingdom of Satan has no fear of a fully battle dressed soldier with no bullets or at best blanks. Prayer is your communication line to the King. The enemy has no fear of your church attendance. But they tremble at the sight of you in the communication center listening to the instructions of the Holy Spirit. It is of the utmost importance for the enemy to isolate us from the communication of God. The enemy knows the same scripture we do, "I am the vine; you are the branches. If a man remains in me and I in him, he will bear much fruit; apart from me you can do nothing" (John 15:5 NIV). In order to be found in Christ, we have to have a relationship with Christ. In order to have a relationship we have to have communications! The enemy knows if they can cut off communications, then they can pull you out of the vine, and apart from Christ we are not a formidable foe.

It amazes me how the children of God run from the study of prayer. We flock to every other kind of seminar found in the church. But let a prayer seminar be offered and the attendance will be sparse if even a handful of people show up. The Wednesday night prayer training usually is the smallest attendance of all the services. Most churches have even got away from prayer training on Wednesday night because of this fact. The enemy's tactics in this area of prayer are obviously working because to be honest most pastors are hesitant to bring in a prayer seminar.

Listen carefully to what is about to be written. ALL of the other information in this book is useless without a working knowledge of prayer. This is the second most vital part to success in our endeavor of spiritual warfare. The first was that of pursuing the study of God's word. The second is the open uninhibited line of communication to the King. I want to take time here to issue the ammunition needed to defeat the enemy. We will discuss the purpose of prayer, and the principles of prayer, before we proceed to the second part of the scripture in Eph. 6:18.

Prayer, as with everything that is spiritual, must have its roots in the worship of God. "All things were created by him, and for him" (Col. 1:16). The purpose of prayer should be first and foremost for the glory of God. Prayer is not simply a means by which we make our requests known, but in a wonderful, far-reaching way, through prayer God is acknowledged, honored and glorified.

Prayer should be looked upon as a means of ministering to God and a channel through which He may minister to us. There is no real prayer if we do not see God upon his throne, reigning with unquestioned sway. We must touch his scepter and receive his mercy and profess him as our rightful Monarch, Sovereign Ruler and Salvation. Where God is truly known, He is always known as supreme. Prayer acknowledges honors and worships Him as such.

The reason we pray and God responds to our prayer is so that God may put His glory on display. Prayer is not for our benefit first, but first is to acknowledge God, glorify God and commune with God, all else flows from that. Prayer that is God honoring is Satan defeating. "That the Father be glorified in the Son" (Jn.13: 31), this is the scripture that gives meaning, purpose, and direction to prayer. It should help us to realize that real prayer begins with a desire to glorify God. We see this truth in Jesus' teaching on prayer. He started the prayer with "Our Father who art in Heaven" Thus He started by acknowledging God as exalted above everything.

We should follow His example and honor and worship God as such in our prayers. Jesus ends by saying, "For thine is the kingdom, and the power, and the glory, for ever. Amen." In the very act of directing prayers towards God we are cooperating with grace in unveiling the glory and presence of God. It is the grace of God operating in us that inspires us to pray. Through our prayers we unveil the presence of God, and thereby His glory will shine through. The first discipline of prayer should be the desire of the soul to acknowledge, honor, and glorify God by faith through prayer. When we bring to prayer the attitude of mind, which looks only to the glory of God, we have a prayer that is perfect. "Who have I in heaven but thee? And there is none upon earth that I desire beside thee" (Ps 73:25 KJV). Do we want God's glory or just God's gifts? I believe we can now see that the beginning and ending of prayer should be the desire to glorify God.

We found the first reason to pray was to glorify God. The second reason is for fellowship. "After this manner therefore pray ye: Our Father which art in heaven, Hallowed be thy name" (Matt. 6:9 KJV). The essence of prayer is based on establishing and maintaining a relationship with God, His church and others. Look at what Jesus said in His prayer. He said "Our Father," which signifies that God is our father too, and He wants a relationship. If a proper relationship is lacking, God is under no obligation to answer prayer. A longing for fellowship with God is the engine that propels prayer. The moment we respond to God's grace and direct our worship, thoughts, and desires back to God through prayer, a sense of God's presence is felt and fellowship is strengthened. Where there is to be fellowship there must be correspondence. Prayer is the correspondence that puts us in touch with heaven and earth, God and man. Prayer increases our awareness of God and others, and awareness is the life of fellowship. Prayer is an expression of love, concern, caring, and a desire for the good of others. This is the lifeline of fellowship.

The next purpose for prayer is that of finding the will of the Father. "And he said unto them, When ye pray, say, Our Father which art in heaven, Hallowed be thy name. Thy kingdom come. Thy will be done, as in heaven, so in earth" (Luke 11:2 KJV). The need of the hour is prayer. Intelligent, persistent prayer gets results because it calls God to action according to His will. It would not make sense to pray if we do not seek God's will and ask for His will to be done. The will of God is described as good, acceptable, and perfect and cannot be improved upon (Romans 12:2). Prayer is the greatest aid we have in doing God's will, and the desire for God's will is a great motivation to pray. Much too often our prayers are only expressions of our desires and of our will, and we hope God concurs.

There are two aspects to God's will, and one response. The first is that aspect of His will, which has already been revealed in His written word, which applies to every Christian. The second aspect involves those decisions in which God has given no specific instructions. The majority of God's will for your life involves the first aspect. If we obey the first, the second will follow. The first thing in seeking God's will is to believe He directs. Second be willing to do it. Our response is to obey where He has already been specific.

The way to peace and happiness is in finding and following God's will instead of our own or the world's. The life from God has a primary demand and that is we should walk according to His will. The very first question we should ask after our conversion with the Lord is "what shall I do Lord." This should be followed by a commitment of "not according to my will, but according to your will." From that day forth, in deciding our future or in choosing our way, it must be laid before the Lord and His guidance sought. Since God wants us to do His will, surely he has and will reveal it and enable us to understand it.

Effective prayer believes that the will of God is more important than our own preferences, proprieties or worldly desires. We do not pray in order to bring God's will into line with ours, but we pray so our will is raised to a level at which God's will is accepted, followed, loved, and desired. Three things are involved in finding God's will. They are the teaching of the Bible, the teaching of the Spirit, and the teaching of God's providential leading. We need to study and pray about all three.

Another purpose for prayer is fighting evil. "O LORD God of our fathers, art not thou God in heaven? And rulest not thou over all the kingdoms of the heathen? And in thine hand is there not power and might, so that none is able to withstand thee" (2 Chr. 20:6 KJV). "If, when evil cometh upon us, as the sword, judgment, or pestilence, or famine, we stand before this house, and in thy presence, (for thy name is in this house,) and cry unto thee in our affliction, then thou wilt hear and help" (2 Chr 20:9 KJV).

When we pray we should be conscious of three aspects of prayer: To whom we pray, for what we pray, to whom we pray against. All prayers, which come from God, will affect the powers of evil. When we seek God's will through prayer it will unquestionably affect Satan, and he will naturally come against your prayers (Daniel 10:12–13). Prayer is a very effective weapon against evil. It is both an offensive and a defensive weapon and should be used as such.

Let's look at prayer as a defensive weapon. We can claim protection for the body against weakness, disease, or accident (James 5:13–16). It is a defense weapon for the mind against deceit, delusion, and discouragement (Mark 1:32–39). It can be a defense for the spirit against bad moods, jealousy, hardness (Ps. 51:10). Lastly, it can defend the will against paralyzing fear or crippling indecision (Ps. 27). Prayer can bring defense for any phase of life. Daniel when threatened with death because of a demand to recall a dream of the king and to reveal its content solved a humanly impossible problem with prayer (Dan. 2:14–23). He wanted to know God's plan; and by praying, he received an answer (Dan. 9).

Prayer can also be an offensive weapon. Often secret prayer is related to public action. Waiting upon and for God, we get our plan of attack. Prayer is vision unfolding God's purpose for life and service. Prayer is often the secret of inspiration. Strength, courage, and endurance become ours to fulfill the divine purpose as we pray. It will benefit you to meditate upon some of the great "fighting" prayers of the Bible, those of Asa (2 Chr. 14:11), Jehoshaphat (2 Chr. 20:6–13), Hezekiah (Is. 37:14–20), and Nehemiah (Neh. 4:9). Paul calls prayers a lance (Eph 6:18). With a lance a soldier could attack his enemy from a distance, in hopes of avoiding hand to hand combat. Prayer unleashes all of heaven to engage in the battle. In essence we affect situations from a distance.

Prayer is God's way to obtain his promises, power, will, salvation, and all that pertains to the Christian life, and the kingdom of Heaven. If prayer is asking then, the answer is obtaining. "And whatsoever we ask, we receive of him, because we keep his commandments, and do those things that are pleasing in his sight"(1 Jn. 3:22 KJV). Prayers that follow the biblical principles of prayer will always obtain results. No Christian should be content until they can be in such close relationship with God that they can obtain that which they have prayed for.

PRINCIPLES OF PRAYER

ASKING

Ask, and it shall be given you; seek, and ye shall find; knock, and it shall be opened unto you.
Matt 7:7 KJV

If ye then, being evil, know how to give good gifts unto your children, how much more shall your Father which is in heaven give good things to them that ask him?
Matt 7:11 KJV

You want something but don't get it. You kill and covet, but you cannot have what you want. You quarrel and fight. You do not have, because you do not ask God.
James 4:2 NIV

If ye then, being evil, know how to give good gifts unto your children: how much more shall your heavenly Father give the Holy Spirit to them that ask him? Luke 11:13 KJV

"Ask and it shall be given you." This is to express your inability and God's ability. You should ask boldly and openly as often as possible. Asking is pleading for the supply of a definite need. The Bible always has conditions attached to the promises of God; these conditions must be obeyed before we ask for the promises of the Bible. Obeying and then asking can only bring our true success as Christians and churches. We have great reason to ask in prayer because God has promised to "do exceeding abundantly above all that we ask, or even think." In your obedience ask of your needs and watch God work miracles in your life.

Next our prayers should be pointed. "Give us this day our daily bread" (Matt 6:11 KJV). All the prayers in the Bible are filled with pointed phrases and definite petitions. Don't just ramble in your prayers, get to the point, and make your request known. I hear so many people pray repetitious prayers that never seem to have a point. We seem to always be praying problems and not answers. If you have a problem then God has the answer in His word. Find the answer and pray the solution. Do not pray for example, God help my fear. Pray thank you father for not giving me the "spirit of fear, but of a sound mind."

Our prayer should be selfless. "But seek first his kingdom and his righteousness, and all these things will be given to you as well" (Matt 6:33 NIV). How different our prayer life would be if only we were truly unselfish, if we genuinely thought of God and others first. If we are self-centered instead of God-centered we will pray only to gratify self.

Our prayers should also be one of persistence. "And Jacob was left alone; and there wrestled a man with him until the breaking of the day. And when he saw that he prevailed not against him, he touched the hollow of his thigh; and the hollow of Jacob's thigh was out of joint, as he wrestled with him. And he said, let me go, for the day breaketh. And he said, I will not let thee go, except thou bless me. And he said unto him, What is thy name? And he said, Jacob. And he said, Thy name shall be called no more Jacob, but Israel: for as a prince hast thou power with God and with men, and hast prevailed. And Jacob asked him, and said, tell me, I pray thee, thy name. And he said, Wherefore is it that thou dost ask after my name? And he blessed him there" (Gen 32:24–29 KJV). "Then Jesus told his disciples a parable to show them that they should always pray and not give up" (Luke 18:1 NIV).

What strong incentive we are given to be persistent and persevere in prayer! Jesus urges us to hold on and be persistent until the answer comes (Lk 18:1–8; 11:5–10). What an amazing story Jesus told to convey this truth. We are to pray with the same persistence as the widow. God the father said; Jesus is not like the judge! But we should be like the widow (persistent).

The next principle is to pray scriptural prayers. "Take the helmet of salvation and the sword of the Spirit, which is the word of God" (Eph 6:17 NIV). The best prayer book in the world is the Bible. Nothing is more effective in prayer then praying God's words back to Him. As our inspiration and guide, we should pray over, through, and with the word of God. The Bible supplies both the example for prayer, and the material for prayer. The word helps us to know the mind and will of God. Prayer helps us make it our mind and will. The richest communication you can have with God is through His word and prayer. If prayer is to be a dialogue (two people talking to each other), we should be as attentive to hear God (His word) as we would be for Him to hear us. Praying the Bible is more than just reciting scripture. It is talking to God about and in response to the scriptures (His part of the conversation). Have you been listening, not to hear words but to gain knowledge?

We have opened the ammunition box and examined the first clip being that of prayer. Now I want to turn our attention to the second ammunition clip, that of supplication in the Spirit. Paul told us we should be found "praying always with all prayer and supplication in the Spirit, and watching thereunto with all perseverance and supplication for all saints" (Eph. 6:18 KJV).

Supplication by definition means a strong petition or request. Not only are we to pray with all prayers that we have already discussed, but also with strong petitions for our needs. I didn't say our wants, but our needs. Sometimes we get our wants and needs mixed up, thinking they are one and the same. When in fact they are not. God's word promises only our needs, and not our wants. Sometimes by the grace and mercy of God we get our wants, but make no mistake our wants are not promised only our needs.

Let us now turn our attention to the latter part of Eph. 6:18, "and watching thereunto with all perseverance" (KJV). Paul puts prayer and watching hand-in-hand together. We see them mentioned together in Col. 4:2, "continue in prayer, and watch in the same with thanksgiving" (KJV). Again in Matthew 26:41, "watch and pray, that ye enter not into temptation: the spirit indeed is willing, but the flesh is weak" (KJV).

We should join our prayers with a spirit of watchfulness thus cooperating with God in answering them. Vigilance, as well as prayer, is necessary to the successful prayer life. Watchfulness is to prayer what digestion is to the body. It assimilates and appropriates it. It makes personal and practical that which is observed. How can one know if a prayer is being answered if one isn't watching for the answer? It seems that far too often we pray not really expecting God to answer so we don't watch and the answer passes us by.

The logical question to then ask is what does the soldier look for? I have found there are four things the watchman should be watching for. First we should watch for the enemy naturally. In chapters two and three we exposed the enemy and that kingdom's workings. We should be watchful so we are not caught off guard. Second we should watch for predators. Those that would come to isolate, conquer, and eliminate us from the love of God. Third we should watch ourselves lest we be found asleep at our post. Fourth we should watch for the returning King.

Now you can understand a little of why the disciples wanted to know how to pray. There is a lot involved in prayer. We have but scratched the surface of prayer. We all need to know it, apply it, and live it.

14

Tactics

We shall start our discussion at the point of "what is tactics?" Tactics is the art of placing or maneuvering forces skillfully in battle. This should not be confused with strategy, which involves planning and directing of the whole war or campaign. Satan, the commander of his kingdom, uses strategy in the planning and directing of the war against the saints. The principalities on the other hand use tactics to maneuver their forces in a way to gain victory over the saints. For example, in the Gulf war the generals used strategy in planning the war effort. The individual units such as the air division or tank division used tactics in maneuvering their troops in order to carry out the strategic plan. Tactics are directed foremost towards individuals or families. While strategies are for the most part directed at the collective body of believers that makes up the Kingdom of Heaven or what is called "the church."

You say, are not these one and the same? Yes and no, let me explain the difference to you. The kingdom of Satan is going against the Kingdom of Heaven. This is like the United States going against Hitler's Germany. You set out strategies to defeat Hitler. Now, you aren't going to call Hitler out in the street for a gunfight. You defeat him by defeating his soldiers. So it is with spiritual warfare. We are arrayed against the kingdom of Satan. You aren't going to have a gunfight with Satan. You will defeat Satan by defeating his army. You see the United States strategically planned for the war against Hitler who was the mind behind Germany. However our army tactically maneuvered against what made up Germany, which is the army. In the same way Satan strategically plans for the war with the church (the body of Christ), which is the representative of the Kingdom of Heaven at this time. However Satan's forces tactically maneuver against the individual members, which are called the bride of Christ. Satan strategically goes against the work of Christ, which is the church, where principalities tactically engage the individual that carries out the work of Christ, which are Christians.

Let's look at some scripture that will shed some light on this for us. "Now ye are the body of Christ, and members in particular" (1 Cor. 12:27 KJV). As individuals come together, they form one body. The body they form is the one called Christ. "So we, being many, are one body in Christ, and every one members one of another" (Rom. 12:5 KJV).

The church is Christ, where Christ is the head and Christians are the body. "As Christ is the head of the church, his body, of which he is the Savior" (Eph. 5:23 NIV). Christ being the head gives life to the body by the power of the Holy Spirit. Whereas we, the members, bring animation of the life of Christ for all to see.

Before you can understand the military battle plan I am going to lay out for you, it is necessary to comprehend the following. First, there is a universal church called "THE church." THE church or universal church is all the churches that proclaim the lordship of Jesus Christ. Look at Eph. 3:6, "That the Gentiles should be fellow heirs, and of the same body, and partakers of his promise in Christ by the gospel" (KJV). It is clear all that follow the principles of the King are a part of "THE church." "For as the body is one, and hath many members, and all the members of that one body, being many, are one body: so also is Christ" (1 Cor. 12:12 KJV). That is why we are told to strive for peace among the body. "Let the peace of Christ rule in your hearts, since as members of one body you were called to peace. And be thankful" (Col. 3:15 NIV). Second, we have what is called "a church." "A church' is the church on this side of town or that side of town. It is the individual churches. Each person in "a church" is a member of the body of that individual church, where one is the leg, and another is the arm, and so on. "THE church" works the same way in that this church is the leg, and another church is the arm, and so on.

A king doesn't return for an empty nation, nor does Jesus return for a lifeless body. The king returns for those loyal citizens that make up the "THE church," which are called in scripture "the overcomers." King Jesus will return, but not as a savior. Understand that Jesus is not returning to bring salvation. The church already received Him as savior for He already accomplished this at Calvary. Jesus is returning as a conquering king. A king who by the power of His very word will conquer the fallen world systems under Satan's control. That is why you read in Revelation of Him returning on a white horse. The King went home to the Father to prepare the kingdom. The King is returning to receive unto the Father those loyal citizens to the kingdom.

"In my Father's house are many mansions: if it were not so, I would have told you. I go to prepare a place for you. And if I go and prepare a place for you, I will come again, and receive you unto myself; that where I am, there ye may be also." John 14:2-3 (KJV)

Jesus is not returning to receive unto himself the empty church of religion. He is returning to receive unto Himself those loyal citizens (overcomers) to the kingdom that make up the church. In order to be classified as a loyal citizen of the kingdom we must abide in Christ. In other words, you must have a relationship with the King. In addition we must strive to know the laws and principles that govern the kingdom and follow those in the power of the Holy Spirit. It is having Jesus as Lord, not just savior of your life. That means every moment of everyday you live by the words of the king. You must accept the authority and lordship of Jesus Christ over your life. As Paul says, "I no longer live, but Christ lives in me" (Gal. 2:20 NIV). That is the bride who the risen King is returning for. Jesus isn't returning for those that are church-like or the religious, He is returning for the Christ-like. Listen, to be Christ-like does not mean you know the whole Bible. There is not a Bible scholar to date that knows and understands the whole Bible. Jesus does not judge you based on how much of the Bible you know and understand. He doesn't expect you to know and understand it all. Jesus does however judge us on what we do with what we know and understand. That is why we read "where much is given much is required" (Luke 12:48).

There are many in the church that have a relationship with religion and doctrine, but know nothing of the King. This is like the parable in Matthew 25:6–12, "and at midnight there was a cry made, Behold, the bridegroom cometh; go ye out to meet him. Then all those virgins arose, and trimmed their lamps. And the foolish said unto the wise, give us of your oil, for our lamps are gone out. But the wise answered, saying, not so; lest there be not enough for us and you: but go ye rather to them that sell, and buy for yourselves. And while they went to buy, the bridegroom came; and they that were ready went in with him to the marriage: and the door was shut. Afterward came also the other virgins, saying, Lord, Lord, open to us. But he answered and said, Verily I say unto you, I know you not."

All of the virgins in this parable knew the right things to do. They all knew how to trim their lamps, and were dressed and ready. They all knew the marriage principles, but some didn't have the anointing oil. We have a lot of religious people who know all the right religious sayings, but don't have the anointing oil of the Holy Spirit. They don't know the King!

When we talk about tactics we are talking about the maneuvers of the enemy to steal your oil. Tactics relates to the individual personage of the bride of Christ. Our discussion of strategy is related to the collective body of Christ that we call the church.

What is the strategy of Satan you ask? Let me give it to you in a nutshell and then we will break open the nut to expose Satan's tactics. Satan's ultimate strategy is to put the Kingdom of Heaven on I.C.E. whenever possible. He wants to Isolate, Conquer, and Eliminate the Kingdom of Heaven. The enemy wants to isolate, conquer, and eliminate the life of Christ from individuals, churches, and nations.

The kingdom of darkness carries out this strategy by way of tactics. They maneuver troops in order to isolate Christians from the Bible. They would isolate us from the command center by cutting off our desire to pray. They would isolate us from other solders that would help us, by keeping us from attending church. They would try to isolate us from our family

by way of our sins. Finally they would isolate us from ourselves through guilt and shame.

Once they have us isolated, they press on in battle to conquer. This is accomplished by arraying their troops in such a
fashion so as to conquer the flesh through rebellion. They would
desire to conquer the soul through vain imaginations and philosophies of men. Finally attempting to conquer the spirit by
way of a dead life to Christ.

Upon conquering the soldier of the cross, they intensify the
attack to gain total elimination. They move in for total elimination
of the life of Christ in the believer. They strive for total elimination of the work of the Holy Spirit in the believer, and finally
pushing for elimination of the love of the Father in the believer.

As the kingdom of darkness examines the terrain to be tra-
versed in this war they find three corridors of approachability. In
order to meet the enemy in battle and be victorious, we must also
know the ways in which Satan can get to us. We must know this
terrain well. The kingdom of darkness can get to us by the world,
or by way of self. The enemy itself can also come directly at you
in a frontal assault. So we can say that self, Satan, and the world
are the three ways the kingdom of darkness attacks.

As you will soon discover in our training of tactics, the enemy's
main objective is to instill rebellion in the hearts of the believer.
Our war with this evil kingdom meets at the battlefield of authority. So I feel it is important that we understand authority. We find
at the root of every problem facing the world and man today is
rebellion of some form. Rebellion caused Lucifer's fall. Rebellion
caused Adam and Eve's fall and rebellion still causes us to fall
today. Everything in God's universe is established on authority.
The following confirm this for us, "and upholding all things by
the word of his power" (Heb. 1:3 KJV). The power speaks of
God's work, where the word speaks of God's authority. A better
way of saying it is, God's work is accomplished by the power of
the authority of His word. Think with me about the Centurion
soldier who had a sick servant. In Matt 8:5–10 we read, "and
when Jesus was entered into Capernaum, there came unto him a
centurion, beseeching him, and saying, Lord, my servant lieth at
home sick of the palsy, grievously tormented. And Jesus saith

unto him, I will come and heal him. The centurion answered and said, Lord, I am not worthy that thou shouldest come under my roof: but speak the word only, and my servant shall be healed. For I am a man under authority, having soldiers under me: and I say to this man, Go, and he goeth; and to another, Come, and he cometh; and to my servant, Do this, and he doeth it. When Jesus heard it, he marveled, and said to them that followed, Verily I say unto you, I have not found so great faith, no, not in Israel" (KJV). This soldier knew and understood authority and that gave him great faith. Even though this was a Roman soldier and not a Jew, Jesus still healed his servant. All because this soldier understood the principle of authority.

When I was in the military, I learned and understood authority, so when I came to a fullness of understanding of the love of Christ, I had no problem with obedience. The word of God said this or that, and I obeyed. I viewed God from my military background, which saw Him as supreme commander. I didn't question the orders from the word of God. I simply obeyed. This is where we find the centurion soldier. He didn't question the words, because he understood the authority of the one saying the words.

Adam and Eve should have maintained their obedience and not eaten of the tree of knowledge (right and wrong). Our actions should not be controlled by right and wrong, but governed by obedience. Eve did not need to have it explained to her why she cannot eat of that tree; she simply must obey the command not to eat. Adam did not need the Lord to explain to him why he must maintain the tree of which he could not eat. He simply had to obey the command to tend to the whole garden. Likewise if you disobey and eat of the tree of right and wrong you will surely find spiritual death. However if you find yourself feasting at the table of life, which is the very word of Christ Jesus you will experience life more abundantly.

Picture two armies set for battle. The army on the right hilltop is the authority of God's word. The army on the left hilltop is the principle of rebellion. The valley in the middle being fought for is your soul. Now listen carefully, if your soul residing in the temple is located in that valley; you cannot house and serve rebellion and at the same time claim to support the authority of God's word.

"No man can serve two masters: for either he will hate the one, and love the other; or else he will hold to the one, and despise the other. Ye cannot serve God and mammon" (Matt. 6:24 KJV). If you find that within yourself is a rebellious spirit. If you're rebellious against the written word or the preached word of God; then you might find yourself recruited as a soldier of darkness rather than a soldier of the cross. If you are looking out of the trenches with a this is right and that is wrong mentality, you will find yourself in the war of the issues. For Eve the issue was the serpent. For Adam the issue was Eve. For the serpent the issue was control. The serpent took control personally and acted accordingly. Eve took the thought of being deceived personally and acted accordingly. Adam took the gift called Eve that the Lord gave personally and acted accordingly. Issues always, I repeat ALWAYS, cause us to take things personally. The enemy will overrun the citadel of your soul the very minute you take things personally. I cannot stress this enough, it is extremely difficult to die to self, the minute you let a problem become an issue and take it personally. Once it is personal you do not want to lay it on the brazen altar.

In counseling married couples I hear husbands say: she remembers things I did two years ago and brings it back up. You know why she does this? It is because what you did two years ago she took personally. Once she took it personally, it can never be solved, because it wasn't consumed on the altar and it's still alive in her. So she managed to suppress those feelings for two years, yet she fed them and now it has grown up and shows itself.

I know very well a father who lost custody of his child because he was a Christian. In fact, the Judge said it was harmful for a child to be raised in a one God philosophy home, and if the father would denounce Jesus Christ he would grant him custody. The father refused to do that and lost custody to a woman who swore to never let that child know about God. Over the years that followed, that father had to watch that child be raised in violent homes and even by a mother who later was convicted of crimes against another child. Yet the courts refused to remove the child. The father was asked quite often how he could remain so calm about the situation. The father would always reply, "it's not personal." You see the father understood authority. He knew the gift of that child was not his to possess, but belonged to God. He knew the Lord was faithful to keep that which he had committed and one day would return the gift, but only if he would lay his feeling and emotion on the altar. God wasn't so concerned with the situation the father was in, but rather how the situation would affect the relationship the father had with the King. God is sovereign and could change the situation at any time, but doing so would also affect the father's relationship with the King. Let me put it to you this way, "God can't change your situation until He changes you." If the father had taken it personally and grown bitter and angry that would have carried over negatively into every relationship he had. Because the father laid self on the altar, God returned the gift ten years later. Not only did God return the child but kept him safe in the arms of the Lord all those years. Moses's mother didn't take it personally, but served the one who took her gift, and God blessed her and Moses.

Let's look at how the kingdom of darkness comes against us in these areas of self, Satan and the world.

SELF

Let's start our tactics training with that of self. The enemy will come against self in three areas, and they are the body (flesh), the mind (soul), and the spirit of man. More often than not I find the attack comes in the order of soul, flesh, and then spirit. Let's look at some examples to see the tactics of the enemy at work.

King David makes for a good example in his sin of adultery. Let's look at those scriptures in 2 Samuel chapter 11 together that we may learn. Starting in verse 2 we read, "and it came to pass in an eveningtide, that David arose from off his bed, and walked upon the roof of the king's house: and from the roof he saw a woman washing herself; and the woman was very beautiful to look upon."

When David got up he merely walked across the room to a door that went out on what we would call a balcony. In those days the balcony was part of the roof. Do you think David didn't know there was a bath on the other roof? David picked the house that Uriah the Hittite lived in. Uriah was the captain of David's army.

David didn't wake up and get some fancy to take a walk. Either Bathsheba talking with her servants or the splashing of the water could have awakened David. Now David got up and went out onto the roof, and there she was, that bodacious Bathsheba taking a bath. At this point David had choices. He could die to himself, those feelings and emotions of the flesh that were welling up inside him. On the other hand he could live in the outer court and feed those emotions and feelings. Notice the enemy has already stormed the first corridor in isolating David. We know he had many wives yet we find the enemy has David restless and alone at night.

We find the choice David made in verse 3. It says, "and David sent and inquired after the woman, and one said, Is not this Bathsheba, the daughter of Eliam, the wife of Uriah the Hittite?" We see the first thing David did was ask who's the babe next door? We see rebellion starting to take shape in David's life. Take notice that David didn't wait till the morning to inquire, he got somebody else up right then to ask. The enemy has taken the first hill of isolation and now presses on to conquer the flesh in rebellion. The first victory of the enemy came by way of the soul. The powers had David troubled in his thoughts because he was restless and bothered by something, which caused him to need to be alone. Next David accepted the lustful thought pushed upon him by the powers, which caused him to become vulnerable to the support element called rulers of the darkness. Once David asked somebody else to identify Bathsheba, and go get her; his sin was no longer private.

The person David asks in essence said, "hello! That's Uriah's house, you picked it for him! Obviously, that's his wife! You know the daughter of Eliam." Even after finding this out David in verse 4 still asked her over, "and David sent messengers, and took her; and she came in unto him, and he lay with her; for she was purified from her uncleanness: and she returned unto her house." You can almost hear the principalities of Satan screaming; sweet is the victory! We have conquered the flesh! Sound the battle charge, for we move in for the elimination of the heart of God in David.

The decision that Bathsheba and David made caused a consequence of an unwanted pregnancy. The consequence brought more feelings and emotions for David to deal with. How was he going to tell or deal with Uriah the captain of his army? At this moment David is again given the opportunity to die to these feelings and emotions. David could stop this ball by confessing and repenting to Uriah and God for his sins. Notice the word sins is in the plural tense. David should confess for lusting after Uriah's wife and for following through with those lusts by sleeping with her. This spiritual defeat of David at this moment affected more than just him and Bathsheba. It affected the whole nation of Israel. In light of that information, we are starting to see the tactical value in attacking David.

Through David's sin, the enemy has isolated him from God and the commanders of his army. This isolation brought another target in view for the enemy to conquer. They next went after David's thought processes. David tried to find a solution to his problem through his mental prowess. He tried to manipulate Uriah into sleeping with Bathsheba so as to cover up what David had done. When that didn't work David had him killed by making him go into battle where he knew Uriah couldn't win. That poor command decision affected the whole nation.

Let's not forget about Bathsheba! She isn't little miss innocent as we are led to believe. First notice that she didn't have to agree to come to David. She could have also died to herself and stopped this tragedy. She could have sent word back to David telling him that, she has not been with her husband for a long time due to the battle you have him fighting. She could continue by maybe stating that it would not be honorable for them to meet in such a private way. She could have said a lot of things, but she didn't. Again we see the enemy at work in isolating Bathsheba from her husband for a long period. This allowed her soul to be conquered through vain imaginations. Those vain imaginations caused rebellion in her heart. She rebelled against her husband in not remaining faithful. I believe she knew full well what she was doing. Notice that she didn't take any precautions not to be seen. Why was she taking a bath at a time she knew David would be home? Why did she not have her servants hold something up so she could not be seen? There was no modesty about Bathsheba. Make no mistake she could have said no! She has to accept just as much responsibility as David does for this affair. As soon as David had her husband killed she quickly married David to cover up the pregnancy. She had no problem marrying the man that had her husband killed.

Sometimes we give more credit than is due to Satan's forces for circumstances that we ourselves caused. Those consequences that come from be willing participants in sinful activity. Sometimes all the enemy has to do is isolate and our fallen nature will take over and finish the assault. Paul puts this in such clear perspective for is in the book of Romans.

Let's look together at Rom 7:15–25, "For that which I do I allow not: for what I would, that do I not; but what I hate, that do I. If then I do that which I would not, I consent unto the law that it is good." That is a lot of I do's and don'ts! What Paul is saying, I believe we all can relate to. How many times have you done or thought something that you didn't really want to? And after you did it or thought it, you would say to yourself, why did I do that? Well Paul gives us the answers, "Now then it is no more I that do it, but sin that dwelleth in me." Paul informs us that there is something else driving him to do that which he hates or does not want to do, and it is called sin. Paul tells us that this sin that is striving to control him is coming from his flesh, for he tells us, "For I know that in me (that is, in my flesh,) dwelleth no good thing." Paul continues in his discourse by saying, "for to will is present with me; but how to perform that, which is good, I find not. For the good that I would I do not: but the evil, which I would not, that I do. Now if I do that I would not, it is no more I that do it, but sin that dwelleth in me. I find then a law, that, when I would do good, evil is present with me. For I delight in the law of God after the inward man: But I see another law in my members, warring against the law of my mind, and bringing me into captivity to the law of sin which is in my members" (KJV).

What Paul is doing here is explaining in detail the workings of a triune man. Remember in our discussion of the base of operations we discussed that man is in three parts. We showed that man has an outer-court called flesh or the body. Man has an inner-court called the soul, which is the mind of man. We also have a holy place called the spirit of man. Paul is telling us here that our flesh (outer-court) delights in the law of sin. On the other hand our spirit, which has been indwelled by the Holy Spirit, delights after the thoughts and principles of the Lord. Our inner man called the mind finds itself in the middle of a war between the desires of the flesh and the prompting of the Holy Spirit. It is in the middle of this war, we find Paul saying, "O wretched man that I am! Who shall deliver me from the body of this death?"

The flesh is like a match in that our feelings strike a spark of emotion that is carnal or contrary to the laws of God. In Rom. 8:6, this is called "carnally minded", and that will bring spiritual death. Remember your brain is like a computer in that when your flesh through feelings sparks carnal emotion it is searching your mind for a carnal answer. A carnal program cannot get a spiritual answer for they are not compatible programs. Paul doesn't leave us in this state of destruction, but supplies the answer to our dilemma. He says, "I thank God through Jesus Christ our Lord. So then with the mind I myself serve the law of God; but with the flesh the law of sin"(KJV).

How did Paul get his once carnally minded mind to serve the law of God, and not the law of the flesh? Most Christians find this a difficult task, because we can't escape walking in this old flesh. It's with us everywhere we go. In 2 Cor. 10:3, Paul agrees that "we walk in the flesh," but he goes on to say we do not war after the flesh. The reason for this is because our flesh should be laid on the altar. Dead men can't war! If our flesh has been crucified with Christ and is now dead why are we still acting as if it is alive and well? Why are we listening to a dead person instead of a living God?

Here is how it works. Before we came to Christ, the body, soul, and spirit were dead to Christ. The principalities and powers ruled our bodies by way of the flesh. They would use the desires of the flesh to seduce our souls with carnal or worldly emotion. Our soul would then dictate our actions, and our spirit was dragged along as an unwilling observer continually convicting through our conscience. Paul tells us that to be carnally mind is the same as being against God (Rom. 8:7).

All that is before we come to Christ. Once we come to the saving knowledge of Jesus Christ the Holy Spirit moves in to indwell our spirit. This causes a problem because that which is against the Kingdom of Heaven is still living in the flesh and is not a hospitable roommate to the Holy Spirit. So the Holy Spirit gives self (flesh) its eviction notice. Self has got to go! Remember it should be laid on the altar. This is where the enemy pops up and says wait just a gosh-darn minute you haven't paid your bill yet. Until your debt is paid in full, my brother self can have full access to the temple. The enemy would be right, we owe a debt we cannot pay. As long as you live in the outer-court of self, feeding on your fleshly feelings and the emotions those feelings cause, then you still would owe that debt. Regardless of whether you call yourself a Christian or not. This is why so many Christians live in defeat, because they live to the feelings of the flesh instead of the thoughts and emotions from the indwelling Holy Spirit.

If you are still living to the fleshly feelings and those feelings of the flesh have not been crucified with Christ then you still owe the debt. As long as self lives, you are telling the Lord that you are capable of paying the bill of sin and death. Consequently the Lord is not obligated to pay through daily salvation. As long as you have erected the idol of self in the temple the enemy has a right to that temple. "And what agreement hath the temple of God with idols" (2 Cor. 6:16 KJV)?

Listen, stop making agreements with the idol of self. Stop letting your feelings control your emotional state and dictate your actions. Only by destroying the idol of self can we truly say we have been crucified with Christ. If self no longer lives but Christ lives through me then the enemy must demand payment from Him for the debt. That is where the victory is for Jesus holds the receipt of payment in full. Amen! The blood of Christ frees us from the debt of the law of sin. Through the Holy Spirit we can "mortify the deeds of the body," and no longer have that debt hanging over our heads.

It is in this selfless state that we find Heb. 8:2 coming to life for us. It informs us that Jesus is the "minister of the sanctuary, and of the true tabernacle, which the Lord pitched, and not man." The gift of the Holy Spirit, given by Christ, ministers to our minds by renewing a right spirit within us. His Spirit that indwells our spirit bears witness of us in Christ. Unfortunately we still find Christians living after their feelings of the flesh instead of after the Spirit of God. Those types of Christians without realizing it are living in rebellion to the Kingdom of Heaven and will live under the consequences of their sins.

Despite this fact, God will give us the grace to sustain us through the consequences of our sins. However, very rarely does He remove those consequences from us! More often than not we have to go through them. David and Bathsheba were no different. Bathsheba may have not really been mourning about her husband's death, but she definitely mourned for her son's death. This was a direct consequence of Bathsheba's sin (2 Sam. 12:15). If Bathsheba had no responsibility in the affair with David than she wouldn't have felt the consequences of a lost son. Look at the consequences that followed David. One son raped his daughter, and then another son killed that son.

We are talking about tactics, so tactically speaking where is the army of Satan in this situation? It is a very safe bet that David didn't wake up that night and have a lust problem. The powers or what I call the intelligence element had pushed lustful thoughts into David's mind long before this night. Their intent was to soften up the target. They strive to get David to live to his feelings and emotion of self. The powers injected what Paul calls in 2 Corinthians, vain imaginations. Men are built visual, and the powers know how to inject those images into our minds. You men know what I am talking about, those images that pop up and you say where did that come from and you have to shake it out of your head. They are called vain or vanity because they have no productive qualities about them. Vain imaginations are destructive by nature. The Bible clearly states that the enemy can impute thoughts into the mind of man. For our example look at John 13:2. "And supper being ended, the devil having now put into the heart of Judas Iscariot, Simon's son, to betray him;" (KJV). Here we see the enemy place the thought of betrayal in Judas. Then we read in Luke 8:12, that the enemy can take away thoughts from man so as to keep him from thinking upon them. "Those by the way side are they that hear; then cometh the devil, and taketh away the word out of their hearts, lest they should believe and be saved" (KJV). The first place Satan's forces attacked was the soul of David, which is to say his thought process.

Was Bathsheba immune to vain imaginations, and the mental attack of Satan's forces? Not at all, they just took on a different look. There was a survey done on what men and woman look for in a partner. Men looked for three things in a woman, how she looks, how she looks, and how she looks. Women also looked for three things but they look for how he will treat her, financial security, and finally how he looks.

So for Bathsheba the powers had to affect her emotions and not her visual senses as with David. We know that Bathsheba had contact with David, because her husband was the captain of the host. She had sat at the king's table before. The story tends to lead the reader to believe that this was the first time David saw Bathsheba. I do not believe this was the case. I think David just didn't recognize her. Keep in mind David was looking at a naked woman bathing at night, and I am sure he wasn't looking at her face. Look again at verse 3, "And David sent and inquired after the woman. And one said, Is not this Bathsheba, the daughter of Eliam, the wife of Uriah the Hittite?"(KJV). The person answering David reminds him that this is Bathsheba. This whole answer given to David implies he knows Bathsheba. The servant comes back and says, you know isn't this Bathsheba? David probably look puzzled so the servant drops another clue and says, come on you know, the daughter of Eliam, the wife of Uriah. So we can see there was some knowledge of each other before the bath incident.

We say all that to see how the powers affected Bathsheba. The vain imaginations they injected into her thought life were one of emotional content. Her thoughts were probably ones of: "my husband cares more about the army than me. I am very lonely. David has been treating me very nice lately." Or "the King went out of his way to talk to me." Maybe one of her servants said, "have you noticed the way the king has been looking at you?" Any kind of thoughts of this nature can stir vain imaginations in her. It was the vain imaginations that allowed her to become the trigger that lowered the boom on David. The rulers of the darkness of this world were able to recruit her because of the successful work of the powers.

This isn't just Old Testament stuff here. This is modern day America. Affairs happen all the time to Christian people. When it comes to lust, David couldn't touch modern times. All one has to do is go to the grocery store to have their visual senses bombarded with images that should make all of us blush. The problem is we are so used to it that it doesn't even faze us, or so we believe. It seems that every other commercial on TV has a woman running around in her underwear.

The question we must ask ourselves is what countermeasures can we deploy to defend ourselves? What tactics must we use to defeat the kingdom of darkness when they attack our thought processes? I hear pastors and layman alike say all you have to do is find a scripture that relates to that problem and quote that scripture. If you haven't tried this, or if you haven't figured it out, let me be the first to tell you, THAT DOESN'T WORK! Oh, sure the first time that you quote the scripture you might find some success. However for the long haul, Satan's forces will beat your volition down and you will lose that battle. That's like an alcoholic waking up every day and saying I am a recovering alcoholic. All that does is reinforce the fact that he is an alcoholic. Eventually his determination will fail him. You can tell yourself for weeks, "Lust not after her in your heart" (Prov. 6:25). All that does is reinforce the fact that you're lusting after her. Like that alcoholic, once he took the drink it's a little late to say I shouldn't have taken that drink.

One day I was giving a spiritual warfare seminar in North Carolina and after I had finished a man came up to me and said he had really been struggling with lust. He said he lived in an apartment complex and there was the woman who likes to sunbathe under his balcony. He was finding it difficult not to lust after her. He said he was quoting scripture and it was working. I said oh? He replied with a very serious look; yea, she has been on vacation in Florida all week. Oh, yeah, that's working!

Listen, you are not going to stop the powers from injecting a thought into your mind. But you can stop them from pulling out the hideaway bed and taking up residency there. For most Christians it is like taking a half-filled glass of water and spending all day trying to get the air out of the glass so you can put more water in the glass. Before we can even think about accomplishing this someone hands us another half glass of water. So it is with most Christians today they spend their entire life running from problem to problem trying to get the bad stuff out of their lives. You can quote scripture all day long and you still can't get the air out of that glass. So how do we accomplish this? This is accomplished by simply pouring fresh, new water into the glass. This will force the air to leave all by itself.

The best method for ejecting from our mind those vain imaginations, in fact it's the best method of pulling down any stronghold of the soul is this: get your mind engaged in thinking about a different subject from the Bible. I am not talking about a passage of scripture I am talking about a subject. Let me give you an example of what I mean. Let's say I have a thought of lust that comes into my mind. I instantly know I have to die to myself, and that thought. So I have two choices, one I can quote scriptures in hopes the thought will go away. If I opt for this choice the thought will go away as long as I keep quoting scriptures. The minute I stop quoting scriptures the thought will return sometimes even stronger than before. Some call this holding up the shield of faith. While quoting scripture will build faith it lacks one important ingredient, that of righteousness. Not to mention it makes for sore arms. If you stand in the defensive mode your whole Christian walk, sooner or later your arms will get tired and the shield will fall. Success is better achieved by having not only the shield but the breastplate as well. We cannot gain righteousness by problem chasing only by God chasing. The first choice is better than no choice, but it is not the best choice.

The second choice, which I have found to be better and more permanent, is to engage my mind in the word of God. I would think for example about the Sunday morning message in Hebrews 6:2, and ask myself why is "Baptisms" listed in the plural tense in this passage the pastor mentioned. The sermon may not even have been about baptisms. It could have been on resurrection or repentance. I wasn't listening to feed on regurgitated food from the pulpit. I was listening to gain my ammunition for that week.

I would ask myself why plural, how many baptisms are there? How does that apply to me? Do you see what's happening? I am not stirring the same stagnated problem water around in the glass. I am adding fresh water to my cup. The minute I actively engage my brain with questions it starts searching the files in my mind for answers. I actively engaged my brain on the word of God, and Jesus ministered to my sanctuary by way of the Holy Spirit (Heb. 8:2). The Holy Spirit quickened my mind to things I needed to remember in order to answer the questions.

All of a sudden I am remembering things and messages that I heard weeks, month, and even years earlier. I remember three, four, and five baptisms. Then I have to think about how each one of those applies to my life. While all of this is happening where did my problem go? It's gone, vanished! Just like that glass of water. You add fresh water and the air leaves on its own.

This is even functional for baby Christians as well, because you don't have to know a lot about the Bible to think about the Bible. Just the thought process will stimulate your regenerated spirit to seek more answers. By doing this, pretty soon you will know a lot of Bible. Not to mention it makes reading the Bible way more interesting then just reading it from cover to cover. In fact the Bible will come alive for you and stop being just a history or storybook. Even if at that moment you are not in a position to go find the answers or talk with someone to help get the answers, your mind is provoked into wanting to know. The minute you are able, you will find yourself looking the answer up in the Bible.

What makes this so wonderful is the fact that not only are you gaining knowledge through the loin belt of truth, but you're also building your faith. As you talk with God through the questions you're asking, God answers by way of the Holy Spirit renewing your mind in the knowledge of God (Col. 3: 10). It will feel like you are hearing the very voice of God! Through this process you are in fact building an intimate relationship with Jesus.

Hear me well. This works because God said it works. Look at Ephesians 4:22–24, "That ye put off concerning the former conversation the old man, which is corrupt according to the deceitful lusts; And be renewed in the spirit of your mind; And that ye put on the new man, which after God is created in righteousness and true holiness"(KJV). Do you know whom we talk to the most? That's right ourselves. We talk at a blistering three hundred and ninety words per minute with ourselves. Most of that conversation is corrupt because of our deceitful lust. I can however renew my mind by actively engaging my brain on the word of God.

That creates righteousness in me, and that righteousness brings out a new man in me. Now instead of talking to myself I talk to God through questions. As the Holy Spirit brings things to my remembrance I talk to God about those things.

Romans 12:2 tells us the same thing. It says, "and be not conformed to this world: but be ye transformed by the renewing of your mind, that ye may prove what is that good, and acceptable, and perfect, will of God" (KJV). When a situation or thought comes into your life that requires you to actively engage your brain on the word of God you are being transformed by the renewing of your mind. Remember, we already talked about the mind being a computer with files. This process will reboot those files, or in plain English, put new files in place of the old files.

Through this process happening time and time again, you begin to gain a lot of knowledge about Jesus Christ. That knowledge coupled with the building of your faith grafts us into the vine of Christ (John 15:1). After you do this for a while, you will find that you are not talking to yourself but talking with God. I call this replacing self-talk with God-talk. This is what 1 Thessalonians 5:17 calls "praying without ceasing" (KJV). Another name for this type of prayer is conversational prayer.

Notice when the enemy attacks in the area of self, the battle is not won with one piece of armor. We had to put on the whole arsenal provided by God. We put on the breastplate of righteousness, and secured it with the loin belt of truth. Our left hand took a firm grip on the shield of faith, while our right hand swung masterfully the sword of the Spirit. In the end we find ourselves standing firm in the Rock of Ages through the fullness of salvation. Even though we know this battleground is in the mind, remember this, the evil spirits have no right to intrude on the freedom of your mind unless you give them free access to it. This is not to say they will not try anyway to gain access to it. As long as you exert your free will, as we have discussed in order to combat the tempting thought they would be defeated.

So we find the enemy maneuvers the following units against us in the battle arena of self.

First the intelligence element called powers tries to isolate us with thoughts. Next the rulers of the darkness use people and things to conquer and buffet us. And last the consequence of our own sin life tries to eliminate the life of Christ in us. Utilizing the principles from God's word that have been shared here, we can die to self and successfully gain the victory in daily living.

THE WORLD

We must remember that because of the fall of man through Adam's sin the world has been against God and militant towards man. "The friendship of the world is enmity with God" (James 4:4). That scripture says that our very love of the world is hostile towards God. "The world knew not God" (1 Cor. 1:21). Not only does this world not know God, but it can't receive the spirit of truth (John 14:17). In fact this world according to John 12:31, has already been judged. This fact is the reason Jesus tells us that His kingdom is not of this world (John 18:36).

The most logical place for us to start is what is the world? That may seem like a foolish question. As we shall find out, the world is more than just a big round planet called Earth. The word used in the Bible is *kosmos*, which when translated means, social order. *Kosmos* takes on three different connotations in the Bible. The first connotation is that of the physical planet (Acts 17:14). The second is the whole race of mankind (Heb. 11:38). Third is the worldly affairs and its system of operation (Matt. 16:26). In our discussion of the world we will primarily concentrate on the latter two, since the first is a given.

Let's start with the worldly affairs and its system of operation. We see from the following scriptures that there is a force or mind behind this world system. "Now is the judgment of this world: now shall the prince of this world be cast out" (John 12:31 KJV). "Hereafter I will not talk much with you: for the prince of this world cometh, and hath nothing in me (John 14:30 KJV). "Of judgment, because the prince of this world is judged." (John 16:11 KJV). It would be so wonderful if when you come to Christ the prince of this world would no longer come against you. Can you imagine how crowded the church would be if we could say come to Christ and there will be no more suffering in this life. We know that just simply is not the truth. We can see in the biblical accounts this is not the case at all. You can't look at the history of the church and not find suffering coming into the believers' lives.

We know that the church is by the power of the Holy Spirit building up to its completion in the universal rule of Christ. At the same time His rival the kingdom of Satan is building up this world system to its ill-fated climax in the reign of the antichrist. We readily accept that sin is of Satan, but how ready are we to see that the things of this world are of Satan, and under his control?

The kingdom of darkness is not so foolish as to attack us through blatantly sinful things of the world. Satan's forces know we will flee things such as nightclubs and bars, or other sinful lusts. However, they know we don't have the same reaction to things like social services, education, and medical science. No, these things seemingly demand our approval, even our eager support. There are a lot of things that we find difficult to agree upon as to where the line should be drawn. Make no mistake about this one fact; God has pronounced judgment on them all. The Bible is very clear in that it doesn't say that He judged just this one or that one, but He judged them all, "now is the judgment of this world" (John 12:31 KJV). 1 John 5:19 agrees "that the whole world is under the control of the evil one" (NIV). Not just the nightclubs and bars, that includes welfare, education, science, art, and all that pertains to this world. It is all under the sway of the kingdom of darkness. I cannot stress enough that Satan's kingdom does not oppose the kingdom of Heaven by sins alone. Satan's forces oppose God by any worldly means afforded them. Highlight this next sentence. Everything that is void of the touch of Divine life is resistant and opposed to even militant towards God.

There is a law of reproduction in the Bible that governs all biological nature. The phrase, "after its kind" in Genesis exposes this law for us. Every creature, even mankind bear offspring of there own kind. Spiritual birth however is not subject to the law of reproduction. Christians cannot reproduce Christians! Even if both parents are Christians, that doesn't mean the child will automatically be born Christian. This will require a fresh touch from God every time. This principle carries over into the affairs of man and the world.

Let's look at government for instance. Whenever a government is left to its own devices it will take a natural course away from the sovereignty of God, even one that is divinely chosen, such as Israel. Think back to when the people of Israel wanted to be like everybody else and demanded a king. Even when God gave them this king under His direction the nation gravitated toward the likeness of other nations. When God removed His divine intervention from the nation, it swayed toward idol-worshipping governmental alignment. Look at our own nation of America. Godly men with godly intentions founded this nation, but how quickly it has swayed to ungodly, immoral political alignment. We have become one of the most, if not *the most* perverse nation. We promote a woman's right to kill through abortion. We promote paganism in our schools and idolatry through Earth worship. We have gone from our founding fathers promoting the study of God's word to our present fathers stripping God's word from our children's education.

Speaking of education, most of our historical universities were founded by Christian men who desired to give a Christian based education. As long as those godly men were alive the fresh anointing of God was upon those institutions of higher learning. But as those men passed on, it took only a short time for those universities to go the way of the world. We could go on and on with these examples, but I think we can now see that the whole world lies under the sway of the wicked one. We are then challenged by two worlds, which is to say two positions of authority. It can no longer or should I say it should no longer be a question of where will I spend my eternal future be it heaven or hell. The more pressing question should be where am I in relations with these two worlds today? Do I belong to a world of order that has Christ as its head, or to the opposing world where Satan rules?

We can expedite our understanding of the topic at hand by placing the world into the three categories that most of us already recognize. The three basic components of the world system are social, economical, and governmental. All three of these are diametrically opposed to the Kingdom of Heaven. If you are an heir to the King through the blood of Jesus Christ then all three are opposed to you and the Christian faith. All three of these components are the workings of man, and Satan's forces utilize those systems for their gain.

Numbers have a significant meaning in scripture. For instance we know that the number seven represents God in that it is a perfect number. We also know the number six represents man. I find it interesting that in the book of Revelation, we see the number of man is listed in the form of a trinity, and that being six, six, and six (Rev. 13:18). Look again at the three areas of man, Social (6), economical (6), and governmental (6). Since man has yielded the world up to Satan through the fall of Adam, we find the number of the beast, is that of the number of man in relation to his worldly systems. All three of these areas are designed to put the Christian soldier on I.C.E. You might take a moment to refer back to the last part of chapter three where I shared the differences between the two kingdoms.

SOCIAL

You can smell the stench of rotting decay of our social society. Indecencies ooze out of every pore of American society. The very foundations of our society that our founding fathers so diligently laid are being surgically removed by the advocates of political correctness. The cornerstones of honor, decency, morals, and ethics are quickly being eliminated.

The enemy tactics is to use society to promote an abnormal normality. What do I mean by this? Society now says that our young women have to be half-dead walking skeletons to be considered beautiful. In order to fulfill this lie, young women are forced to accept another lie of self-gratification. They think they have to enlarge this or shrink that in order to have the so-called normal body. We find mothers more concerned with breast augmentation, than with breast-feeding. The enemy has begun to isolate our young woman from the self-esteem building norms of the Bible, and replaced it with the destructive abnormal ideals of society. As magazines, movies, and books indoctrinate our youth, they become easily conquered by insecurity. Then they fall susceptible to elimination through depression and anxiety. These young women look for and crave answers, but the church in most cases doesn't talk about the issues and give sound answers. So these women turn to the world for answers and get them. Even though the answers they get are lies from Satan to them they are still answers nonetheless.

Our society has perpetrated a hypocritical stance on life. Our society has promoted and advocated the theory of evolution and the survival of the fittest. They push the idea that we are all basically animals. I call this a hypocritical stance because when a species of animal finds itself being swallowed up in the food chain of life these evolutionists scream stop, we have to protect them. I think to myself, that's part of your evolutionary theology. How ironic we find them trying to manipulate their own theology to suit themselves! Consequently we have raised a generation that believe they can do whatever, whenever, to whomever they want. I had an opportunity to talk to a teenager during the Y2K ordeal, and I asked him what he was going to do if something happened. He said he would just take whatever he wanted from whoever had it. I then asked, what if they don't want to give it to you. He responded flatly, I would just have to kill them, its survival of the fittest. And society wonders why kids are shooting up our schools.

Society demands we give up the death penalty for child molesters and murders, yet says it is OK to give a woman the right to kill her baby through abortion. Then society wonders why our young mothers are losing their mothering instincts and skills. All of these things, the kingdom of darkness uses to wear down, beat down and suppress the Christian soldier, or cause them to defect to the other side.

Society brings induced stress into the believer's life. Do I have the right clothes, hair, or even car? Remember it's not a matter of heaven or hell it's a matter of which society will I base my norms on, the Kingdom of Heaven or the kingdom of darkness. We should base our society and its intrinsic values on what the word of God says they should be. If we accept man's definition of normalcy, could we have in fact accepted the number of the beast as well?

The spiritual wickedness of Satan's kingdom will use people through their sins to affect the innocent and the Christian alike. My pastor related a story of young women that was abused as a child by her father. My pastor told her that God was there for her and wanted to help her through this pain. The question the young woman posed startled him, as it did me upon hearing it. Her question was this, where was God when she was being abused? Why didn't God answer her cries for help during that pain? The indoctrination from society upon that father caused him to sin. Society says feed your pleasure; there are no morale absolutes. That caused great induced suffering and pain for this young woman. This father's sin has isolated his daughter. The enemy forces also isolated him from his wife, friends, and church because of guilt. The vain imaginations of one man affected a whole family, and if uncovered could possibly affect the whole community. Do you see the strategic value in these targets? The enemy knows how not to waste resources on valueless targets. This example falls under the definition of terrorism, in that the enemy attacked the least number of people (the father), to affect the greatest number of people (the family and possibly the community).

Sometimes the consequences of other people's sins become ours to bear. Think about a husband or wife that has an affair on their partner. That one sin affects two whole families as well as their friends and relatives.

Sometimes the rulers of the darkness (support element) will recruit someone specifically to come against you. This was the case in Job with the Chaldean and Sabeans. I want to take time here to look at two such cases in the hope we shall gain a better ability to see how people are recruited. Also to expound upon a key principal that will give us a greater fortitude and ability to defend against these kinds of attack.

The rulers of darkness in the book of Job were recruiting Job's closest friends. How do I know they were his closest friends? Verses 11–13 of chapter 2 tell us this fact. In those days you didn't just hop into your SUV and dash over to Job's house. It probably took weeks to get to Job's house. When they saw him they wept with him. They showed genuine sympathy for Job's condition. Let's look at these friends for a moment to try to uncover the reason behind Satan recruiting them. First there was Eliphaz the Temanite. Temanites were known for their wisdom (Jer. 49:7). So we find Eliphaz conducts his discussion with Job from an intellectual, human experiential standpoint. The next friend is Bildad the Shuhite. Bildad held his discussion from a traditionalist standpoint. And finally we find Zophar the Naamathite. Zophar argues from the standpoint of human merit. Chapter 4 verse 6 tells us that Eliphaz reminded Job of his fears. Remember Satan's plan (strategy) was to get Job to curse God and die. The tactics used by Satan's army was to rail on him through those that should be bearing his burden. Here comes Eliphaz telling Job, you never were really upright. Your righteousness was all a big act. If that weren't the case than all of this wouldn't be happening to you. In verse 6 of chapter 5 Eliphaz tells Job, isn't this your big fear? That we would find out you are not so upright after all. Have you ever heard that before? You're just playing religion; you're really not holy before God! That's Satan trying to make you give up and let him rule your life again.

In verses 12–21 of chapter 4 we see the combat element (spiritual wickedness) come onto the scene. A fallen angel gives more ammunition to Eliphaz for the purpose of shooting fiery darts at Job. As you read those verses notice some very key phrases that inform us that this is a demon or fallen angel. First "a thing was secretly brought." Nothing from God is secretly brought for it is revealed from the mountaintop. Next, Eliphaz was "trembling in fear" and the angel never said "peace be still" or anything to calm him down. Angels sent from God always said peace be still or something to calm you down. The angel of the Lord wanted you to remember what was told, and that would be difficult with you trembling in you pajamas. That is why we read Eliphaz only remembered a "little thereof," because he was too scared to remember it all. And last the demon told lies. No angel sent from God would tell lies, for only Satan is the father of lies.

The next friend, Bildad, tells Job his condition is his own fault because that is the way it has always been understood. God punishes the wicked, therefore Job must be wicked. This takes place a lot in churches today. The preachers read some commentary and preach it, then someone is told what was preached, and wham instant tradition. Now we have people like Bildad saying that is the way it's always been, or that's what I have always been told. This is like the story of the lady getting ready for a family reunion dinner. Her daughter asked her why she was cutting the ends off the ham. The mother replies, because that is the way her mother did it. The daughter says, well grandmother is here let me ask her why she did that. When asked the grandmother replies, because that is the way her mother did it. Again the young lady states that, great-grandmother is here so let's ask her why she did that. When asked the wise old woman states with a smile, I did that so it would fit in the pan. All of these years they have been throwing away good meat so it would fit in someone else's pan. So it is with churches today, we have been throwing away good meat of the word of God so it would fit in the pan of tradition.

Notice that Job did not accept tradition as truth and neither should we. We should always test what we read and hear to see if the fruits it bears is good. The last friend to speak is Zophar, and he tells Job he's wrong based on his merits. Zophar says there must be sin in your hand or these things wouldn't be happening. Sometimes people say the same to us. They exclaim bad things are happening because you're doing bad things that we don't know about. There are more people in churches today under the oppression of guilt because of this lie from Satan. Remember it is not personal, just business. It is the world's business to beat you down, and you don't always have to have done something wrong to feel the pain of the beating, as it was in Job's case.

Job's three friends railed on Job for days trying to get him to give up. How did Job handle this? Did he yell at his friends, and tell them to shut up and go away? Did he fall down crying, you are right please help me? No, we find no such happenings in Job. Job had on the whole armor of God. In chapter 5 verse 1 Eliphaz asked Job which angel will Job call upon to save him. Listen to Job's answer in verse 8–9, "I would seek unto God, and unto God would I commit my cause: Which doeth great things and unsearchable; marvellous things without number:" (KJV). Job recognized that his friends were being used of the enemy, and in chapter 6 verse 15 he reproves them for their deceitfulness. The key to Job's composure was that he didn't take it personally. Job expected sinful people to act sinful. Job said all of man's life is but a fleeting moment and all his days are filled with trouble. You see it wasn't personal, it was business. It's the world's business to beat man down, and Job didn't take it personally. The minute you take things personally you put a big neon sign up inviting the demon of anger into the temple. Job could have railed back on his friends, but he didn't, why? It was just a problem and problems can be solved. It hadn't evolved into a conflict by becoming personal. Once you take it personally then hate, anger, and hostility creep in and produce sin in our lives. Because Job never allowed that to happen, we are told that in all that he did he sinned not.

Sometimes people have a nature about them that is just malicious. Some people have a personality that makes it easy for the ruler of darkness to recruit them. They are manipulative, deceitful, bitter people. Let's look at such a case in the story of Joseph and Potiphar's wife (see Genesis 39 and chapter 12 of the Koran).

Zuleekha, Potiphar's wife, was very taken with the looks of Joseph. Joseph's looks were celebrated all over the east. It was said that Zuleekha invited forty of the most beautiful women of Egypt over for a party. When they saw the beauty of Joseph, they all said this must be an angel. You might say when it came to looks, Joseph was the Elvis of his day. We learn in this passage that Zuleekha tempted Joseph daily, wanting him to give in to her lust. He always refused her advances. Finally when no witnesses were around she threw herself upon him, and he fled leaving behind the shirt off his back which she was clinging to. She used that shirt to have him thrown into jail for allegedly trying to rape her.

What Zuleekha didn't realize was that the rulers of the darkness of this world were under orders to silence Joseph. Joseph was bringing God into the light of the peoples' eyes. Sometimes the enemy brings people into our lives for the sole purpose of hindering us. This was the case with Zuleekha and Joseph. However, Joseph held the same key as Job. He didn't take what Zuleekha did to him personally. You are probably asking how I know he didn't take it personally? If Joseph had taken it personally, then he would have become vengeful in his attitude. Anger and hatred of Zuleekha would have infected his insides. Joseph would have been screaming at his jailers: "let me out I've been framed. I'm innocent I tell you. That good for nothing, lying little witch, Zuleekha did this." That is how people react if they have taken it personally. We don't see that response from Joseph. If we had, the keeper of the jail would not have looked favorably on Joseph. The keeper would have said, "man, will that Joseph ever shut up about Zuleekha?" Even after Joseph got out of prison years later and saved all of Egypt; he didn't use his power to come against Zuleekha. He had forgiven her before he was even put into prison.

Sometimes the very people you worship God with will be recruited to execute you with their words and actions. We must learn the lessons of Job and Joseph and look not at the person committing the offense but rather what is behind the person using them. The old saying, "hate the sin and not the sinner" rings true. This can only be accomplished by not taking things personally. The world tells us to lash out and get even with our enemies. That is exactly what happens when we fail to die to self; we end up taking things personally. The word of God on the other hand tells us to love those that hate and hurt us. Remembering the real enemy we are to hate is the army of darkness. Only by accomplishing this can we demonstrate true righteousness before men.

ECONOMICAL

If people aren't being used to buffet you, then the army of Satan will use economics to rob you and your family. They will rob your family of time. We have this function and that meeting demanding our time. They keep us so busy doing so-called good things that we fail to have family time as commanded by God's word. I have even seen God's people so busy doing "the ministry" that they fail to include the first ministry of the home. If you are so busy that you find it difficult to adhere to the word of God, then you have accepted the way of the world. If you no longer find time to pray to God or study the word of God, be careful, for in the world is the number of the beast. The world would tell us that we need money, and must we have more. As we work harder and harder to meet that demand the enemy's isolation tactics begin.

The world tells us we have to have more—bigger, nicer cars, and large, luxurious houses. They would have us to believe we need lots of money and toys. It seems that most people today, including Christians, have fallen out of love with Jesus to return to a love of the world. Because of our love of things, we have become so in debt that over 70% of the people in churches fail to be obedient to the simple command of tithing. Over 80 % of churchgoing people fail to pray on a regular basis. God's word tells us,

"What good will it be for a man if he gains the whole world, yet forfeits his soul? Or what can a man give in exchange for his soul?" (Matt. 16:26).

Economics drives us to work overtime, and two, or sometimes three, jobs just to have what the world says we should have. But I ask you at what cost have we done such a thing. In Matthew 13:46, "the kingdom of heaven is like a merchant looking for fine pearls. When he found one of great value, he went away and sold everything he had and bought it"(NIV). Are we eager to give away those fine things for the joy of the Kingdom of Heaven? Or again, do we find ourselves locked in the talons of the number of the beast?

There is probably nothing more difficult than doing business in an honest and straightforward manner in today's competitive commerce. However, God demands that we use His principles in every area of our lives including business. Many a businessman has used their businesses to profit the Kingdom of Heaven. As J.C. Penney said, "If a man is too busy to worship God twice on Sunday and once on Wednesday night, he has more business than God intended him to have."

We find that Satan was the first businessman in that he traded ideas for his own gain. Even before this we find Satan in the business of trafficking merchandise. "By the multitude of thy merchandise they have filled the midst of thee with violence, and thou hast sinned: therefore I will cast thee as profane out of the mountain of God: and I will destroy thee, O covering Cherub, from the midst of the stones of fire" (Ezek. 28:16 KJV). "Thou hast defiled thy sanctuaries by the multitude of thine iniquities, by the iniquity of thy traffick; therefore will I bring forth a fire from the midst of thee, it shall devour thee, and I will bring thee to ashes upon the earth in the sight of all them that behold thee"(Ezek. 28:18 KJV). We must follow God's principles in all things including economics.

The kingdom of darkness uses man to bring about the whole arrangement of things on Earth that we have become entangled in. We cannot find one of us immune from its touch.

This is why we should daily cry out to Jesus for salvation from the world systems. We should be found daily wearing the full armor of God, and carrying all the weapons given to sustain us.

What every Christian should remember is that we are strangers in this world, and that our citizenship is in the Kingdom of Heaven. Most Christians look at the Kingdom of Heaven as a take it or leave it kind of proposition. Nothing could be further from the truth. Peter tells us in 1 Pet. 1:18–21, "Forasmuch as ye know that ye were not redeemed with corruptible things, as silver and gold, from your vain conversation received by tradition from your fathers, But with the precious blood of Christ, as of a lamb without blemish and without spot. Who verily was foreordained before the foundation of the world, but was manifest in these last times for you." We can see from this scripture that all of our things cannot save us or bring lasting joy and peace. We also see that the traditions of our fathers, no matter how good they might have been, cannot save us or give lasting peace.

Only the precious blood of Christ can save us as we see in the next scripture. "Who by him do believe in God, that raised him up from the dead, and gave him glory; that your faith and hope might be in God. You see all of our faith, hope, joy, and peace comes from my identity with the risen Savior." I should not say, I am looking forward to Heaven, but in the meantime I will get as many things as possible, so I will be happy. Isn't that what most Christian's are doing? I find my happiness in the joy of the Lord regardless of whether I have things of this life or not.

Governmental

The last part of the world that we will discuss is that of the governmental. It is very obvious to any honest observer that the government is under the sway of the kingdom of darkness. All one has to do is look at what is being pushed at us by the government and what is being stripped away from us to see the truth of the matter. We shall see how Satan uses the government in a big way in the strategies chapter.

Kingdom of Darkness

We have looked at how self comes against us. We discovered a little about how the world comes against us. Now I want to turn our thoughts to the frontal assault of Satan's army. The enemy will use anything it can as weapons to attack us. We must know the enemy's devices. Equally important is to know our own strengths and weaknesses that could be used against us.

As we have already discussed the enemy wants to I.C.E. the life of Christ. In order to do this they must first bind up that which gives animation to the life of Christ, the body! You being ambassadors, representative of the life of Christ, the enemy must bind you up. To do this the enemy is going to as they did with Job, conduct some background checks on you. They will know your strengths and weaknesses. They will assess the strength of the word of God in your soul (loin belt of truth). They will determine the depth of your relationship with the King (breastplate of righteousness). They will test the fortitude of your trust in the King (shield of faith). They will test your stamina on the battlefield of life (shoes of preparation). Above all they will hinder the lines of communication with the King (prayer and supplication).

Knowing that the enemy is going to check and test these areas, is it not important that we check ourselves in these areas as well? We need to do what I call a self-threat assessment. I need to know what my strengths and weaknesses are, so that I can maximize my strengths and minimize my weaknesses. Let me use myself as an example. I am a very structured organized goal oriented person. Those qualities in themselves are good. The enemy also knows my weakness. I am not a very tolerant person. If someone asks me a question, I will answer with the truth, even if the truth is not really what they wanted to hear. Those of you who are married know that can be a dangerous thing. The enemy can use those strengths against me. The enemy does this by using my weaknesses. Being conscious of this weakness, I need to continually pray for strength and guidance in letting Christ rule that area of my life.

This area of rebellion is the area of first attack for the kingdom of darkness. If they can get you to revolt against the word of God, or perhaps cause you to overthrow the workings of the Holy Spirit in your life, then they can isolate you.

My wife told me of a time when she felt like she was being guided to invite someone to lunch in order to help him or her. She felt they where sad or depressed, but then she would say to herself; I don't have the money. Satan used her weakness of economics to hinder her from being obedient to the authority of God. Her identity at that moment was in her pocket book and not in her Savior. Once she discovered that was a weakness, she never let money stand in the way of her being obedient to God, and has felt the blessing of that obedience ever since.

Once we have made an honest self-examination of our strengths and weaknesses, we can proceed to the best part of spiritual warfare, which is predicting what the enemy is going to do. Once you have donned the breastplate of righteousness, and securely fastened the loin belt of truth. Upon methodically lacing the shoes of preparation, and securely latching the helmet of salvation. Once you have the whole arsenal of God, then you are ready for battle because knowing the enemy's movement demands battle.

Start by keeping a very simple daily journal. Nothing difficult or lengthy! Simply write down when you rise in the morning how you feel—whether you feel good, sad, joyful or however you feel. Then at lunch again write down how you feel. If it has changed, think back and record in your journal when and why you believe it changed. Then at bedtime again write down how you feel and, if it has changed, note when and why. After about six weeks you will start seeing some patterns start to develop. For example every time you wake up happy you will find yourself running into the same one or two people that cause your mode to change.

A lady I knew tried this and told me every time she got up happy she ran into the same lady that just got under her skin. As the days passed, she grew to hate to even see this lady come around and went to great lengths to avoid her. That is not doing battle! That is called running from battle. This wonderful Christian lady said to herself, here comes that Mrs. Plankhead, I better run the other way. What she wasn't realizing is that the powers knew how to ruin her happy mode, and the rulers recruited Mrs. Plankhead to become the spiritual wickedness to do the job. You see Mrs. Plankhead wasn't her enemy! In fact Mrs. Plankhead was a victim in the same battle. The real enemy was the powers and the rulers of the kingdom of Satan.

So what is this Christian lady to do? How is she to defeat this unseen enemy? First, by recognizing who the real enemy is and attacking that enemy. Next this lady should run towards Mrs. Plankhead instead of away from her. If she gets up this morning happy she knows Satan is going to recruit Mrs. Plankhead to ruin her day, so she should pray.

She should pray, "Lord, I know Mrs. Plankhead is going to come around today, so please give me love and patience towards her. Lord, help me to show you to her today. So I pray right now, that you will guide her into my path today that you may be glorified." That will cause the enemy to put up or shut up! The enemy is going to have to move on Mrs. Plankhead to avoid you because the enemy doesn't want Mrs. Plankhead to know the love of Christ. Once you realize that this person is not your enemy and that you are both in the same boat; that you are both being attacked by the same enemy, it becomes easy to love that person.

Once you start seeing the patterns emerge, you can then start looking at what element of Satan's kingdom is coming against you. Knowing this will help determine what tactics you will need in order to defeat them.

15

Strategies

To the intent that now unto the principalities and powers in heavenly places might be known by the church the manifold wisdom of God, Eph. 3:10 (KJV)

We have already stated the ultimate strategy of the kingdom of darkness is to put the Kingdom of Heaven on I.C.E. Since the Kingdom of Heaven is made up of those individuals that are born again and striving to be Christ-like, we can say Satan's force would desire to put born again Christians on I.C.E. In the last chapter we talked about how the enemy accomplishes this through tactics. What I want to concentrate on in this chapter is how the enemy comes against us collectively as a body of believers, and what the response of the church to those tactics and strategies should be.

If we can agree that the strategy and tactics of the kingdom of darkness are targeting the church called Christ's body; then we must also agree that there is very high tactical value assigned to the church. We are told in Matt. 12:29 "how can one enter into a strong man's house, and spoil his goods, except he first bind the strong man? And then he will spoil his house" (KJV). In order to steal your homes, communities and nation Satan has to bind up the bride of Christ. If there is a godly individual in the home, Satan must first bind that individual up before he can spoil the house. If there are godly individuals in the community, then they must be bound up to steal the community from the love of Christ. So it is with a church, or nation.

Keeping this in mind we must remember that there is a war going on and act accordingly. We must consider that the church is on militant grounds or else Satan's forces will gain an advantage over us. Now I am not advocating anyone run out and start bombing anything. "For our struggle is not against flesh and blood, but against the principalities, against powers, against the rulers of the darkness of this world, and against the spiritual forces of evil in the heavenly realms" (Eph 6:12 NIV). Our battle, as clearly stated in scripture, is not against flesh and blood, but against the kingdom of darkness.

Because of the fact that most churches fail to realize the gravity of the battle, the leadership finds they are trying to prepare for battle after the enemy has already begun the attack. The church should have already been an equipping center for the training and preparedness of God's soldiers. If we would only adhere to the command to know the wiles of the devil, then we would not stay in the defensive trenches all the time. The assessment of the enemy should always be in the mind of the church leadership and the watching of the enemy's movements always before their eyes.

It is like the scenario from the first page of this book. If a terrorist group was attacking churches and the government said you're on your own. Would you not make preparations to defend yourselves through assessment of the enemy? Would you not keep their movement in view through observation? In the spiritual warfare before us, not only has the government said you're on your own, but in most cases has been recruited to help the enemy. To be ignorant of the battle is to have lost before we even begin to fight. "My people are destroyed from lack of knowledge" (Hosea 4:6 NIV).

Victorious churches win first in strategy and then go to battle; while defeated churches go to battle and then try to implement strategy. Listen, the kingdom of darkness has set up far-reaching plans and are patient in implementing those strategies. They look for just the right moment to strike, in efforts to gain the most from the victory. On the other hand churches have near-sighted plans with poorly constructed strategies, and we wonder why we are defeated before we begin. Don't get me wrong, I agree we have lots of long-range plans to build a big new building. We have long reaching plans to add wonderful programs. But we have very few, if any, plans to aggressively attack the kingdom of darkness and return that which has been stolen from the King. We are heirs to the King, yet we are so easily persuaded to relinquish our inheritance to the enemy. Spiritual warfare is a war that will be won not by might, but by wits. Might only sustains conflicts, but strategy wins wars. We get those wits from the renewing of our minds with the word of God.

The enemy thinks very strategically in their war with the saints. The church, to be victorious, must also begin thinking strategically in its war against the kingdom of darkness. Let me give you a living example of this battle. I will use my neck of the woods to show all the strategies of Satan and the countermeasures that should be deployed.

Satan looked at "the church" in the nation of America and said, "where is the strongman or stronghold?" The answer is: in the Bible belt. That must be bound in order to gain a foothold in this nation. For our example, I want us to consider one city in the Bible belt called Asheville.

Asheville is a beautiful place nestled in the mountains of North Carolina. At one time Asheville was largely a Christian community. As of late it has become quite the opposite. Most people cannot tell you when it changed. It was like they woke up one day and it was different. *Rolling Stones* magazine calls Asheville the "freak capital of America." Asheville is now called the new age Mecca of the world. It is said that per capita Asheville has more homosexuals and lesbians than any other city in America. What happened to this Bible believing community? I believe the same thing that is happening all across the Bible belt. The enemy is strategically eliminating the life of Christ by binding up the church. The political correctness propaganda machine says we are becoming diverse. However, as we shall see, their idea of diversity is a one-way street leading to lawlessness. Remember, the mind behind the world's systems seeks to manipulate events to its advantage.

If you were to make a timeline chart of all the events that led to the change in this city, you would see what made the change— sort of a city diary of daily events. For the enemy to gain control of this Christian city called Asheville, they had to begin an insurgency. The enemy must begin to convince the people that their system of ideas and philosophies are wrong and the authority over them is unjust or nonexistent. In a nutshell, they say there is no God, or at best your God is unjust and narrow. The tactic of choice the enemy uses is terrorism. They use coercion, intimidation, and fear to move people to their way of thinking. The big victory for the enemy is to get the general public to believe its way of thinking.

The first thing to happen was the enemy started recruiting the media in order to have a way of spreading its propaganda. The local paper swayed from its primarily Christian view to a humanist, worldly view. Oh! They sprinkled enough Christian thoughts in so as not to make themselves too obvious, but to an honest observer you can see even those thoughts were written to put Christ in a bad light.

Once the media objective had been reached, they turn their attention to key city officials that they could recruit to implement their policies. If there are none that can be recruited at this time, they will recruit some that will run for office next time. I know you are probable thinking, come on, the kingdom of Satan is capable of all that! Most definitely, YES! The word of God shows us this fact in the book of Daniel. You remember the story in chapter ten. This is where the principality of Persia held up Gabriel from bringing the answer to Daniel's prayer. Gabriel told Daniel when he goes back and helps eliminate the principality of Persia that the principality of Grecia would take over the area of Persia. Every war fought, whether won or lost is a direct result of the heavenly battles. Well in that story we were given a behind the scene look at what goes on in the world.

Now let me give you the reality of that battle. At about 336 B.C. a war broke out between the king of Greece who controlled the area of Grecia, and the king over the area of Persia. The king of Persia had a full navy, hundreds of thousands of soldiers as well as fifty thousand Greek soldiers hired with their generals. The king of Greece had only seventy-five thousand soldiers. The minute the principality of Grecia took over the area of Persia he brought his human puppet with him. Because of this change in power in the heavenly sphere, we see thirteen years later Alexander the king of Greece conquered the area of Persia. That king of Greece later became know as "Alexander the Great."

This is what's happening today in that principalities try to control the world systems by and through people. Let me see if I can paint the big picture for you. The enemy wants to push its ill-fated kingdom forward. To do this they need to push towards a one-world government and economic system. The enemy has tried to do this many times before in human history, most of the time it has been through war. This was the case in the day of Caesar of Rome, Napoleon, Alexander, and Hitler.

In William L. Shirer's book *The Rise and Fall of the Third Reich,* he tells of the men who influenced Hitler's philosophy and ideologies during his rise to power. One such man was H.S. Chamberlain. Shirer's book explaims how Chamberlain by his own admission was "given to seeing demons who drove him to seek new fields of study and to get on with his prodigious writings." Shirer's book goes on to say, "These demons drove Chamberlain to get off a train and shut himself up in a hotel room for days writing a thesis called race and history." This demon-possessed man called Chamberlain had a large influence on the rise of Hitler.

Satan was not allowed to gain world domination through any of the war efforts of these men. It is through these failed attempts, that the enemy, I believe, learns a very valuable lesson. You can catch a lot more flies with honey than you can with a bullet. We see the new revised strategy working in America today. You control the world by money, not force.

Strategy number one–*get the people so tied to money that they will do anything to keep it.* Look how indebted we are as a nation and as individuals. Even in the church, we find Christians so tied to money and things that they have failed to be obedient in the area of tithes and offerings. Over the last few years plastic money called credit cards are being shoved down America's throat. For a newly-married couple to have a twelve hundred-dollar house payment is common. They even add to that a four hundred-dollar car payment. Then you add living expenses and presto you have instant division in the family. It now takes both parents working to make ends meet. The number one problem in marriages is money. This also means their kids are left alone or to someone else for a large part of the day. Not only does the enemy have mom and dad separated for a great portion of the day, but also has the school systems raising our kids to think the way the government wants them to think.

Humanism is the only religion accepted and taught in our school systems today. Even the Supreme Court decision of Torcaso *vs.* Watkins acknowledges the fact that humanism is a religion. Listen to what the *Humanist* magazine in 1983 stated. "The battle for mankind's future must be waged and won in the public school classroom by teachers who correctly perceive their role as the proselytizer of the new faith; a religion of humanity utilizing a classroom instead of a pulpit to convey humanist values in whatever they teach." From 1983 to now we can see the effects of the humanist propaganda pushed on our kids. We find rape, murder, drugs, and all forms of lawlessness running free in our public schools.

Strategy number two–*gain total control of the people.* To accomplish total control they first must take away any measure of self-defense, and self-reliance. The senate is trying to pass a bill that would give law enforcement agencies the right to search and seize property without a warrant. Long before this bill, the senate had passed a lot of gun regulations. That way they know who has guns and who doesn't. You need to know, before you search someone's house, whether they have a gun or not. Right here in the little town of Asheville, the health department sent out a "Student **Health** Center Questionnaire," that asked students about any firearms in the home. I still find no reason for asking such a question on a *health* questionnaire other than to gain information on who owns guns. When the health department was asked about the question their response was, "they drafted it from the American Medical Association." Gun control is nothing new to world domination. Hitler passed gun regulations in Germany so they could control the people. The government tries to get the people to rely on the government for their everyday needs. We now find the government regulating and controlling every facet of our lives.

Strategy number three–*limit both the church's ability to grow and its sphere of influence into the community.* Here in Asheville the city redefined the word Church. In 1997 the city slipped in a new definition of the word "Church." Instead of the usual definition of a "tax-exempt institution, devoted solely to religious purposes;" it now reads that a church is "a place where religious worship is conducted. The term church shall not include day care, educational, recreational and other facilities which are incidental to the place of worship." That definition strongly limits a church's sphere of influence now doesn't it? Just look at China, Russia, and Germany, many nations have tried to limit the church, if not totally wipe it out. Satan knows you have to bind the strong man called "the church" no matter what nation you are in. Asheville saw many policy changes that affected the church in a negative way. So Asheville saw the enemy was successful in recruiting key city officials.

The next step in the enemy's take over was to bring many new people into Asheville with views contrary to the Christian faith. Every gay and lesbian magazine ran invitations to those individuals to relocate to Asheville, as did every new age and humanist magazine. It wasn't long before the norms started shifting. What once was wrong is now considered right, and what once was right is now considered wrong. The best way to defeat an opponent is to make their forces useless without firing a single shot. That is what the enemy did when they shifted the norms for Asheville. Satan's army forced the church to eat of the same tree as Adam and Eve, the tree of right and wrong (knowledge). If we fight on the grounds of right and wrong we will find ourselves caught up in the battle of issues. This will cause us to use the wrong weapons of fleshly emotions. We will engage the wrong enemy of flesh and blood. The flesh instead of the Spirit will drive our motives. It is not a matter of right vs. wrong it is a matter of obedience vs. rebellion.

The enemy knows the hardest thing for Christians to do is die to those emotions and feelings that the tree of right and wrong brings out in us. They know if they can stir the emotions that cause us to get angry, then they can throw us into lawless confusion. This strategy causes the church to fight the wrong enemy. We end up fighting issues instead of Satan's kingdom. Fighting issues causes us to fight people and sometimes even ourselves in the process. Issues quickly become personal for most people and once the issue becomes personal, they more often than not will harden their hearts to what you have to say. Let me again give you an example of one such campaign. Satan had its puppet called the Supreme Court remove student led prayer from football games. Satan knew that he could easily persuade the general public to his way of thinking on this issue. Satan knows it will be hard for the church to prove something has really been taken from them. So weeks before the ruling from the Supreme Court, Satan's recruited media promoted the idea that Christians are emotional nut cases that need to be silenced at best, or ignored at worst.

That strategy was effective for the enemy because the church did get angry with that issue calling it the "last straw." This is like a story of a Chinese general who after returning to his camp from battle saw the enemy drawing near to encourage another battle. The Chinese general refused to come out to fight. The enemy showered his camp with arrows. Those arrows landed right next to the general, but the Chinese general sat calmly. At that point his captains remarked, we could easily take this army. The wise general replied no, this army is from far away and short on supplies. That is why they push for a do-or-die fight. The best choice is to remain calm and wait.

The kingdom of darkness rained arrows at the church. Instead of the church remaining calm about this prayer issue, and making long-range strategic plans, the church got angry and set out on a "We Still Pray Campaign." Listen carefully when I say this was not a bad idea or wrong to consider such a campaign. What I am saying is the way this campaign is waged was and is strategically short-sighted and can be easily defeated by the enemy because it was carried out in an angry response to the arrows of Satan.

Let's look at this campaign from a strategic standpoint. Since we know the enemy's strategy is to sway public opinion away from the life of Christ and bind up the voice of the church. We must counter that by swaying public opinion back to the truth of Christ. With that being said, did this campaign sway the unsaved of the community toward the truth of God's word? In short, NO it did not! Sure there where thirty-five thousand Christians from all over this area who came to a rally, but that shows that we helped Satan's kingdom stir the emotions of Christian's which fed into Satan's hand. He wanted as many Christians as possible angry with this issue, because that would further show what the media had been promoting for months leading up to this battle: that Christian are emotional nut cases. Next, Satan knew exactly how the church would react to this issue and had patiently laid long-range plans to use the church reactions against them. Let me quote some facts to show you how predictable the church is to Satan's army. The *Asheville Citizen-Times* newspaper received a letter in October from a northern-based printing company. The company president stated that they were changing their minds about relocating to Asheville because of the "We Still Pray Campaign." You would think the local paper would have printed that letter right away, but it didn't. The paper held on to it for three months, and then made it a front-page issue on December 28th. The newspaper stated that Lawrence Erlbuam the president of this company heard of the "We Still Pray Campaign" from a magazine called the *New Yorker*. The casual reader is led to believe that this president who was considering relocating his company happened to read an article in a magazine and that caused him to change his mind. There was however a fleeting quote that told the real story. The paper reported Erlbuam as saying he "visited Asheville several times and had talked to someone he knew very well and asked for help in scouting locations." The question that needed to be asked, was who was this person Mr. Erlbuam knew in Asheville, and were they a part of the movement of the enemy in Asheville.

It was very easy to find out that Mr. Erlbuam didn't really want to relocate his company to Asheville. First clue is he said he was going to employee two hundred workers in Asheville, yet his company to date only has one hundred employees. Next clue was he did not go through normal channels that any company wanting to relocate would go through. He did not notify the Chamber of Commerce or inquire with the city about room or taxes.

The enemy knows that a lot of jobs have been lost in Asheville because of NAFTA. So two hundred more jobs not coming to the area because of Christians would be a very large bullet fired at the church. The kingdom of darkness also knows that most people won't go through the trouble to find the truth, but instead they will believe what they read in the paper. In addition the enemy knows it will cause an angered reaction in the Christian community as well as with the leaders of the "We Still Pray Campaign." That anger will cause the Christians as well as those leaders to react out of emotion rather than reacting from the love of the Spirit.

The church is predictable, because that is exactly what happened. The paper immediately went to the leaders of the "We Still Pray Campaign" and said what do you think about that? Because there was no long-range strategic plan in this campaign it was easy for the enemy to again stir the festering pot of emotions. If there had been long-range strategic plans laid, the leadership of this prayer campaign would have known what the enemy could have done and prepared responses to those actions. Is this possible? Most definitely, YES! If this were not the case then we would not be commanded to know the plans and schemes that the enemy uses. Paul would not want to keep the enemy from gaining an advantage of the church because the church is ignorant of Satan's devices (2 Cor 2:11).

As I have observed and participated in this war of the kingdoms, what I am about to write I do with love and a pure heart. In order to expose the enemy and gain victory in this fight I am compelled by the Holy Spirit to write this part. I have wrestled extensively with how to leave this part out and still expose the enemy, and I have come to the conclusion that it can't be done. So please remember that if I step on your toes, I am stepping on mine as well for we are all one body.

One leader of the prayer campaign took this as a personal assault against the prayer campaign. He went so far as to call the president of that company causing the conflict to escalate even more. Here is the response another prominent leader gave to the paper when asked what they thought: "I think he's the loser for making a snap judgment about our community, it is a very tolerant community." Even though the spokesman didn't say anything that Asheville hadn't already known, it was a good response in that it didn't make railing accusations against the enemy. The community knows it's tolerant, but believes that the church isn't tolerant. This response does nothing to counter that opinion. Keep in mind we are trying to counter Satan's strategy of swaying the general public's opinion. What makes this response good is the fact that it appears he didn't take this issue personally and responded accordingly. If he did take it personally, he was able to die to those emotions and feelings, and not use his influence before this newspaper and lash out at Mr. Erlbuam. He did however point out the Asheville paper's irresponsible journalism. A little later down the road the Asheville paper made him pay for that statement with even greater irresponsible journalism propagated against him.

A better, more strategic response, would have been: "We hate to hear about this company's decision. Obviously Mr. Erlbuam's company is not diverse enough yet to relocate to a city such as Asheville. Maybe in a few years when this company has matured he will reconsider." Did you notice what I did? I threw the same terminology of diversity back on the enemy. You know that reporter is going to say, wait a minute how can you say that? Mr. Erlbuam's company has Jews, Muslims, and a whole range of diverse peoples working for him. Then you could respond by saying that is true however Mr. Erlbuam does not have any Christians working for him. So his company isn't that diverse now is it? Or are you saying that diversity is a one-way street and that street isn't accessible to Christians?

Now if you could respond that way calmly and in love you would have crawled out of the defensive trenches and on to the battlefield. You would put the principalities controlling Asheville on the defensive as well as sway the public opinion with the truth.

One leader of the "We Still Pray Campaign" took this issue very personally and used every means possible to lash out at not only Mr. Erlbuam but the unsaved community as well. Look at his response as quoted in the Asheville paper. "[This leader] questioned how serious Erlbaum was about an Asheville location, saying Erlbuam simply wished to criticize the We Still Pray Campaign." All that statement did to the unsaved community was cause them to say; see the We Still Pray group is trying to blame that company for not bringing two hundred job to Asheville. Even though the leader spoke the truth, it was a truth that needed to remain silent for now, because the reaction it would cause in the unsaved community would not be beneficial to the Kingdom of Heaven. Remember this isn't about an attitude of me; it is about the Kingdom of Heaven. Does your statement make the King look good or bad?

The leader continued by stating, "Anybody that would feel unwelcome because the Lord's Prayer is spoken at a ball game is a little narrow-minded." That statement made the unsaved angry and they took it personally. Because they took it personally they hardened their hearts to the Christian voice. This statement escalated the fighting and did nothing to sway the unsaved towards the truth of Christ.

As if that statement wasn't bad enough, he was quoted in the *Asheville Tribune* as saying, "Christians only move on emotion and there is a need to get their emotions moving." That statement told the community that the church agrees with what the media has been pushing for months and that is Christians are emotional nut cases that need to be silenced. I want to shout NO! Christians need to be Spirit driven and not emotionally driven. Has the church gotten so lazy that instead of training people how to die to themselves daily, we use their emotion to fight conflicts that are for all intents and purposes not winnable. His emotional statements were more damaging to the Kingdom of Heaven than anything Satan's forces had done.

Should the "We Still Pray Campaign" be thrown out just because it was not strategic? No! It should have made long-range plans to win this battle, which I don't believe was done. If we wanted to awaken Christians to the changing policies on prayer at ball games, then we won this battle. If however, we wanted to deal Satan's kingdom a fatal blow on this issue, then we lost miserably. Did we sway the public's way of thinking on this issue? No! Did we get prayer back in ball games? No! On the other side we did strengthen the enemy's position in the community by our response. The "We Still Pray Campaign" is pushing for a change in legislation, which is a good thing, and did make Christians aware of the problem.

If you were to lay out a map of Asheville and its surrounding area and then mark with a pin all the churches that have split or had pastor problems you would see a pattern. This is what is called spiritual mapping. When I spiritually mapped the Asheville area, I found the enemy's strategic battle plans were laid out before us. The first objective was the downtown area, which the enemy easily conquered. Once they set up their stronghold downtown they moved out to the surrounding area.

The number one reason the kingdom of Satan is so successful against the church is because churches have become so detached and alienated from each other. We have become spoiled brats spiritually. Unfortunately the responsibility rests solely on the leadership of churches. I have heard pastors say, I will not fellowship with that pastor or church because they don't read the King James Version of the Bible. Anything and I mean ANYTHING that causes division among the body of Christ is straight from the pit of Hell! That statement says the man in China who was saved by reading one page of the New Testament Bible that was smuggled in to him is no longer saved, because that page came out of the New International Version. Think about this: does your relationship with Christ change because this other pastor uses the New International Version and not the King James Version? If you fall into this category, I am sorry, but repent!

As long as my brother over here or there believes in the fundamental truths of God, then I must fellowship with them. As long as they believe that Jesus is the Son of God, the Bible is the inherent word of God, and the resurrection of the saints, then I can fellowship with them. It will not change my relationship with the King if I agree with speaking in tongues or not. I don't have to agree with every little doctrine of every church in order to have fellowship with them. It is clear from scripture that the churches that believe in those fundamental truths are all part of one body.

This concept of becoming one is the first thing you learn in basic training after enlisting into military service. They force a dozen or more people of different backgrounds to work as a team or become as one. When one member of the team hurts all of the team hurts. The sergeant in charge would say if one of you were going to do push ups, you all were going to do push ups. At first the team would get mad at the one and try to make them quit so the pain would go away. That however brought stronger discipline and more pain from the sergeant. It didn't take long to learn the best course of action was to help the one succeed.

This is one lesson the church has failed to learn. Every church is a part of the same team. If one church is hurting, we all hurt. It is like when your feet hurt, your whole body hurts. Are you going to cut off your feet because they hurt? Certainly not! You try to soothe your feet till the pain goes away. What if when a church splits for whatever reason it reduced the tithe by over half in every other church in a hundred-mile radius of that church. Would we then begin to understand the idea of one body? When the pastor of the church four miles down the road falls victim to the enemy's attack through adultery or gambling or whatever, most churches think, great we are getting ready to grow. That is like amputating your right arm and your left arm saying great I am getting ready to grow. That sounds stupid because it is stupid! Churches think they are doing so well because they are growing, but don't stop to realize they are growing at the expense of the other parts of the body. We move members around from one body part to the other, but really don't grow from outside the body. The legs feed off of the arms and the arms feed off of the eyes and so forth. We should grow from the outside and not from within. We should go out to the highways and byways saving the lost, and then bring them into the body to be trained and nourished from the word of God.

We are told in Eph. 4:3–4, to "endeavor to keep the unity of the Spirit in the bond of peace. There is one body, and one Spirit, even as ye are called in one hope of your calling." We must become one body. As long as the kingdom of darkness has us divided we cannot stand against his wiles. We should not let our little differences divide our greater common bond in Christ. If your sister church down the road has split or the pastor has left because of sin then every church in that area should help heal that church. All of the pastors and staff of those other churches should get together and help their hurting sister church. Each month one of those churches could send an associate pastor or youth pastor to bring the messages for that month concentrating on restoration and healing. At the same time another church might send worship teams to lead music to help restore joy and peace. It is hard for the music team in that hurting church to feel worshipful. At the same time another church might have an on staff counselor that they could send to counsel those that are hurting and in need. The desire of all the churches in that area should be to help that one hurting church from losing one member because of the problem. Not only should we desire to help keep them intact, but also we should strive to help them grow. The reason this is so important is because God has given each church a specific vision and mission that meets a need in the community. Every church doesn't necessarily have the same vision and/or mission. When Satan's forces can Isolate, Conquer, and Eliminate (I.C.E.) a church in the area he has come one step closer to putting your church on I.C.E.

Only when we can accomplish this bonding in peace can we engage the enemy on the battlefield. If we cannot find a common ground with those that are filled with the love of God how can we ever expect to deal with those that are opposed to God? If we cannot show as commanded in Ephesians 4:2, "all lowliness and meekness, with long-suffering, forbearing one another in love," how can we ever show those things to the principalities and powers as commanded, let alone to a dying, lost world.

ENGAGING THE ENEMY

In order for me to lay out the strategic battle plans of the Kingdom of Heaven we must understand some things. First, what is the true purpose of the body of Christ? Most people think it is to save the lost. Let's see what the word of God says on this subject. Looking at Eph. 3:10, we find "to the intent that now unto the principalities and powers in heavenly places might be known by the church the manifold wisdom of God" (KJV). We can see from this scripture that the purpose of the church is to show the manifold or complete wisdom of God to the principalities and powers. Notice it did not say, show the wisdom to a dying, lost world did it? Jesus told his disciples in Matt. 28:19-20, "Go ye therefore, and teach all nations, baptizing them in the name of the Father, and of the Son, and of the Holy Ghost: Teaching them to observe all things whatsoever I have commanded you: and, lo, I am with you always, even unto the end of the world. Amen" (KJV). Again He didn't tell them to go and save all nations. He said teach. Jesus knew the battleground is in the soul (mind) of man so he wanted to replace the bad files in the mind with good files from the knowledge of the word of God. This scripture implies we are to teach that Jesus is more than a savior. It implies we are to teach that Jesus is Lord and King. Verse 20 is saying teach them to follow the King's authority in all matters. We are told that Jesus "came to destroy the works of the Devil" (1 John 3:8). Walking in the knowledge of the salvation of Jesus alone does not destroy the works of the devil. However walking in the power and authority of the word of God, by way of that salvation does destroy the works of the devil. Do you understand the difference? One says I put on my salvation face on Sunday morning. The other says every moment of every day I am under the Lordship and authority of Jesus Christ. In order to continue what Jesus started in destroying the works of the devil, we must train God's people in the principles that govern the Kingdom of Heaven.

I will use Asheville again to show the battle plan for destroying the works of the devil. We know the strongman has to be bound up first in order to steal from him. That works against Satan's forces as well as against us. In Asheville the stronghold is in the downtown area. That is where the principality has set up his command center. Like any war anywhere in the world the first thing you must achieve is air superiority. We know from Eph. 2:2 that Satan is called the "prince of the air," meaning he has control or air superiority. So the first step is to take back the air from the principality. I know you are thinking, come on that is stretching things a little! Not really, think back on Daniel when he prayed and the principality of Persia held up the answer for 21 days. That principality had air superiority until Michael came and helped Gabriel gain air superiority.

AIR SUPERIORITY

So how do we gain air superiority? Very simply by prayer! The fervent prayer of one righteous man will prevail over all principalities. One man's prayers are better than a million rallies. The churches in Asheville should come together and set up intercessory prayer teams that would pray over the downtown area for seven weeks.

OPERATION P.U.S.H.

I call this prayer bombing, or operation P.U.S.H., (Pray Until Something Happens). Those prayer teams would pray very specific prayers. They would pray for the spirit of God to move over that area softening the target for the word of God to be accepted. They would pray for the ungodly businesses to be convicted of their ways, and every person entering those businesses would be convicted as well. They would pray for the godly businesses to prosper in that area. They would pray for the sphere of influence of the churches in that area to increase.

During this seven-week prayer bombing the pastors and leaders of the churches in the Asheville area should get together with the pastors and leaders of the downtown churches. All of the churches should find ways to help the downtown churches because those churches are getting ready to grow immensely. These downtown churches may need teachers, nursery workers, and music leaders. They may need help with printing or other material needs. All of their needs must be met during that seven-week period before the next phase of battle begins.

OPERATION OVER RUN

The next phase of battle is called operation over run. We must over run the enemy's stronghold and putting feet to our prayers does this! In the second phase we would help those downtown churches print and pass out flyers and leaflets. We might even think about conducting or bringing in some seminars to those churches that would affect the community. To the godly businesses that we had been praying for, we would send a card or letter letting them now we are praying for them and appreciate them maintaining their Christian stand in today's business world. We might even send a letter or card to every member of City Council letting them know we are praying for them and our city. We would send a card or letter to every fireman, policeman, and schoolteacher in the downtown area letting them know we are praying for them. The way I would suggest doing this is to assign each intercessory prayer team so many people to pray for. You would divide up all the places and people that need to be prayed for evenly among the intercessory prayer teams. Then those prayer teams would write the letters or send the cards. That will create a more personal touch that has a more powerful effect.

It is always good to pray! However in most cases the ones you are praying for never know you are praying for them. By putting feet to our prayers we are letting them know we are praying for them. We are also reaching out to them in a personal way offering help and restoration. We offer help for their needs and restoration for their rebellion against a Holy God. Rebellion covers every sin issue, whether it is homosexuality, abortion, drugs, or any sin, it all falls under rebellion against God. You see I don't have to fight against that homosexual all I need to do is help him deal with his rebellion. I do this first with prayer then through compassionate sharing of the truth of God. The minute I come against his homosexuality, it becomes a personal issue for him and that is a battle that, more often than not, will be lost to the Kingdom of Christ. You cannot win battles at the tree of right and wrong. That is why Adam was told to stay away from it. You win battle through the obedience to the tree of life. Hear me well, homosexuality is a sin and will destroy your life. But is homosexuality any greater or lesser of a sin than lust, greet, adultery, and abortion? NO, they all carry the same sentence of death. It is not about homosexuality, it's about rebellion against God. Mr. American male, it's not about you cheating on your wife, it's about your rebellion against God. Doctor Abortion, it's not about the thousands of babies you have killed, it's about your rebellion against a Holy God for the love of profits. Do you see the common denominator of rebellion?

What if you went to the doctor with the flu and he only treated you for the cough and sore throat; in essence he only treated the symptoms and not the cause of those symptoms, would you ever get well?

So it is with sins! If you chase sin issues then you are only doctoring the symptoms and not the very cause of those symptoms. That is a battle the church can never win! We must go after the very root cause in order to eradicate the effects. Eliminating rebellion against a Holy God is a battle that can and indeed must be won. In order to be victorious I believe we must begin to do three things. First, American churches need to think unity in the bond of Christ. We need to unify the body of believers in order to stand strong. Second, pray like we have never prayed before. Pray with an eager, excited, anticipation of seeing God do what He said He would do when His people pray. Third, think strategically and act tactically against the kingdom of darkness.

Conclusion

I encourage all believers to put on the full arsenal of God. Stand ready to avenge all disobedience with our readiness to obey. I encourage all Bible believing churches to unite under the bond of Christ Jesus, our Lord and Savior. For the love of Christ Jesus, begin to work together for the glory of the Kingdom of Heaven. When these things are accomplished they can say, truly the Kingdom of Heaven is at hand. Above all let joy abound in your soul for the knowledge that we are but pilgrims in this land, and the King of Kings is returning for His bride.

May the peace of God be with you as you endeavor to run the race set before you!

Your fellow soldier in Christ,
T.J. Dillingham